Russian Agriculture

In the

1880s

By

William Bosch

Acknowledgements

I thank my family and friends for their support and encouragement while I was writing this book. I am especially grateful to the members of the German-Russian community for their interest and moral support.

I am indebted to the authors and cartographers who produced the text and beautiful maps and diagrams in the original copies of Industries of Russia, Volume 3. They did a remarkable job considering the technology they had available at that time. I give credit to them for their maps and diagrams throughout this book.

I also thank Stephen Babbitt, Professor of Mass Communications at Black Hills State University in Spearfish, SD for helping me design the cover and formatting it.

William Bosch
November 2016

Other books by this author:

The German-Russians in Words and Pictures

Table of Contents

This page left intentionally blank

Preliminaries

The Purpose of This Book

In 1893 the World's Fair: Columbian Exposition was held in Chicago. The Russian Government brought a large number of materials and books to that fair. One such book is called The Industries of Russia: Agriculture and Forestry, Volume 3. A more complete citation is given in the references. Hereafter, we will use the abbreviation IR to refer to this book.

Besides the Preface and Introduction, IR contains twenty-two chapters on the status of agriculture, forestry, fisheries and rural industries in the Russia Empire at that time. Much of the data is based on the years 1880–1892. The Russian and English versions of IR were published in 1893 in St. Petersburg.

IR contains 37 maps and 10 diagrams (we might call the latter charts or graphs). Most of those maps and diagrams are in color and are loaded with interesting information about Russian agriculture in the 1880s.

I have examined three of the original English copies. The first was an interlibrary loan from a major university. That copy was in poor shape — the binding was loose and some pages were detached. I sent it back and started looking for a copy to buy. I finally found one and paid $200 for it before finding out the Introduction had been cut out. This copy too had a lot of loose pages. Later I found another in somewhat better shape for $50. I have seen a third copy advertised for $300. Based on my small sample, I would say the original copies of IR are scarce, expensive and in poor shape.

However, there is some good news about gaining access to the narrative part of IR. It is available on-line courtesy of Google. The URL is: https://books.google.com/books?id=_dZDAAAAYAAJ&dq=The+Industries+of+Russia,+Volume+3&source=gbs_navlinks_s. ULAN Press has also reproduced it with the title The Industries of Russia, Volume 3, and copies are available at

Amazon.com for about $34 at this time (late 2016). A complete citation for this work is given in the references.

These reproductions are scanned copies of the original. So the pages of each correspond exactly to the pages of the original. The text part of each looks good and is very readable. But the maps and diagrams are of poor quality or missing entirely. I invite you to go to either reproduction and look at the map just prior to page 97 of the text (Chapter VI. Breadstuffs, Map No. 8). Note that the color tabs in the legend are either white or very dark and hence useless. In the reproduction by Ulan Press, the diagram just after page 104 (Chapter VI. Production of Grain, Diagram No. 4) is a blank page with just a smudge down the middle. Moreover, the name of Chapter VI is Breadstuffs, even in the original. It is not "Production of Grain".

Here is a quote from the back cover of the ULAN Press copy:

"While we strive to adequately clean and digitally enhance the original work, there are occasionally instances where imperfections such as blurred or missing pages, poor pictures or errant marks may have been introduced due to either the quality of the original work or the scanning process itself. Despite these occasional imperfections, we have brought it back into print as part of our ongoing global book preservation commitment, providing customers with access to the best possible historical reprints."

IR is in the public domain in the United States. It may seem that a solution to obtaining good images of the maps and diagrams is at hand. Why not just scan the 37 maps and 10 diagrams from the original copy? Unfortunately, this does not resolve all the issues.

The colors in the original copies have faded and, in some cases, are sloughing off the pages. So even carefully scanned copies turn out to be less than sharply outlined and colored. Even if the color of the copies was excellent, that would not take care of all the problems. As I pointed out previously, the name of Chapter VI in the text is Breadstuffs. But in Diagram 4 of that chapter it is called Production of Grain.

Here is a sample of other problems with the maps and diagrams in original copies of IR:

Chapter VI. Breadstuffs. Map No. 14. This map is labeled Map No. 12 in IR but it is the second Map No. 12 and it comes after Map No. 13. Hence it should have been numbered 14. Also the numbers for Zhitomir were placed over that name and are very hard to read. The same is true by Moscow as the numbers are placed over the name of the Oka River. Problems like this abound throughout the maps and diagrams in IR.

Both Maps No. 1 and No. 2 in Chapter X are titled "Total Number of Cattle." But the legends say the maps give us the "Number of large and of small live stock per 100 inhabitants" and the "Number of large and of small live stock per 100 dessiatines of fertile soil", respectively.

Map No. 1 in Chapter III has a number of areas colored incorrectly. And a number of maps use archaic notation such as 2,3/4 instead of 3,75 or 3.75.

Crawford, in the Preface to IR, gives a reason for these oversights and mistakes:

"As in the Preface to the volumes on Manufactures and Trade, I beg again to remind the reader that this entire series of volumes on The Industries of Russia, for the World's Columbian Exposition, covering in the Russian nearly 1,900 pages, large octavo, has been prepared in the greatest possible haste, so hurriedly in fact that it has been impossible to avoid important errors both in the original and it its translation into English."

After taking all of these issues into account, I was led to the conclusion that these maps and diagrams have to be redone completely. The beauty of the maps and diagrams, the importance of the data displayed therein and the cultural and historical importance of the whole book demand that the maps and diagrams be preserved in a format that is as readable, attractive and error-free as possible.

So in late 2015 and early 2016, I reconstructed these maps and diagrams. A version of each one appears in this book. I broke some of them into two in order to adequately display all the information. I tried to eliminate all of the errors and defects but I am sure I missed some and added a few new ones. Any remaining errors are my responsibility.

I added narrative to provide context and explanations for the maps and diagrams. This book is useful by itself or as a companion book to one of the reproductions mentioned earlier.

The Organization of This Book

IR contains an introduction and 22 chapters. The titles of the chapters in the rest of this book are the same as in IR. For each chapter, I provide a section called **Highlights** and a section called **Remarks.**

In the highlights I give quotes or narrative on the important or interesting parts of that chapter. Naturally, my own biases come into play in making those choices. In order to help you understand my viewpoint, here is a brief summary of my background.

My father was born in 1898 in Crimea near Simferopol in the German village of Rosental (now called Aromatne). He was brought to the United States the following year. My mother was born in the United States.

Both sets of my grandparents were born and grew up in what is now Moldova, Ukraine and Crimea. The areas in which they lived are relatively close to the Black Sea. My ancestors are of German ethnicity and were invited to Russia by edicts promulgated by Catherine the Great and Alexander I. They migrated to Russia around 1800. Eventually large numbers of German colonists settled along the Black Sea and Volga River. Shortages of land and a deteriorating political climate caused many of these people to emigrate to the Americas in the late 1800s and early 1900s. They are known as German-Russians in the western hemisphere. Large numbers of German-Russians settled in North and South Dakota, Nebraska, Kansas, Canada and in other areas of the United States as well as in South America. I was born in Linton, North Dakota and grew up on a nearby farm.

Thus my primary interest is how people lived and worked in southern Russia in the late 1800s. Of course, people living in southern parts of Russia influenced and were influenced by people, conditions, politics and events in other parts of European Russia. So in selecting highlights and making remarks, I tried to be balanced and objective.

Even though each chapter has a remarks section, if immediate clarification seemed wise, I did not hesitate to make a remark in the highlights section. In the highlights, I wrote as if I was living in the 1890s and used the present tense. So if the authors of IR said that cotton was no longer as important in 1890 as in previous decades I wrote "Cotton is no longer as important now as it used to be in previous decades."

However, in the remarks section of each chapter, I revert back to the present time and place. In those sections I make whatever comments may serve to clarify or make connections with statements in the highlights part. I also point out pertinent additional information in other chapters of IR or in other sources.

Maps, Diagrams, Units and Conversions

The authors of IR used a variety of units of measurement such as dessiatines, chetverts, versts, arshines and others that are no longer used in Russia or elsewhere. Some maps and diagrams use both those historical Russian units as well as English units such as acres and bushels. Currently most countries of the world use the metric system with hectares, kilograms and so on. It would be too expensive to render and print each colored map and diagram in three ways using the old Russian units, the English units and the metric units.

So I tried to choose units based on historical interest and current usage. Where appropriate, I make suggestions on converting from one set of units to another. IR and the reproductions of it contain a long list of Russian units and their English equivalents on pages XIII–XV which you may wish to consult. This list is more extensive than any I have found elsewhere.

Names and Places

European Russia is the part of Russia west of the Ural Mountains. In the 1880s it was made up of the 50 regions listed in the first part of List A below. Map A below shows those 50 regions as well as the other areas enumerated in List A. This map is the background map for all maps in IR and in this book. I added the names of Odessa and Volgograd to the base Map A. Otherwise the names and boundaries are identical to the maps appearing in IR. The black curve on Map A will be explained in Chapter II.

Map B gives another view of the 77 Russian Governments in the 1880s. Political subdivisions in Russia are called Governments. They are similar to our states or provinces. List A also contains governments in Finland, Poland and the North Caucasus because they were part of Russia at that time. The numbers in List A correspond to the numbers on Map B.

The names on list A are the capitols of the governments shown on Maps A and B. The names of capitols usually coincide with the names of provinces but not always. For example, Kishnev was the capitol of Bessarabia. In List A, the names in parentheses are the names of the provinces used in the text part of IR.

We should also keep in mind that names can have different spellings in other languages, sources and time periods. Kishinev is also spelled Chisinau or Kishinyov and is now the capitol of Moldova. Sometimes in IR a variant of a name is used to refer to the inhabitants of a town or region much as Americans might call Denver residents Denverites or Texas residents Texans. Usually the context will help you understand how a word is being used.

Unless you are very familiar with Russian Governments and geography, you may want to refer to List A and Maps A and B as you read this book or a reprint of IR. Another useful map for this purpose can be found at https://www.zum.de/whkmla/histatlas/russia/russia1880s.gif.

After List A and Map A and Map B, we begin the highlights and remarks for each chapter of IR. The names of succeeding chapters of this book are identical to the chapter names in IR as recorded on the first page of each chapter. The Index of Contents and Authors in IR (their "Table of Contents") has, in some cases, expanded titles for the chapters.

List A

European Russia:

1. Archangel (Archangelsk)
2. Astrakhan
3. Chernigov
4. Ekaterinoslav
5. Grodno
6. Kaluga
7. Kamentz-Podolsk (Podolia)
8. Kazan
9. Kharkov
10. Kherson
11. Kiev
12. Kishinev (Bessarabia)
13. Kostroma
14. Kovno
15. Kursk
16. Minsk
17. Mitau (Courland, Latvia)
18. Mogilev (Moghilev)
19. Moscow
20. Nizhni-Novgorod

26. Penza
27. Perm
28. Poltava
29. Pskov
30. Reval (Eastland)
31. Riazan
32. Riga (Livonia, Livland)
33. Samara
34. Saratov
35. Simbirsk
36. Smolensk
37. St. Petersburg
38. Tambov
39. Simferopol (Tauride)
40. Tula
41. Tver
42. Ufa
43. Viatka
44. Vilna
45. Vitebsk

21. Novgorod
22. Novotcherkassk (Don)
23. Petrozavodsk (Olonets)
24. Oriol (Orel)
25. Orenburg

46. Vladimir
47. Zhitomir (Volhynia)
48. Vologda
49. Voronesh
50. Yaroslav

Finland:

51. Abo
52. Helsingfors
53. Kuopio
54. Nicolaistadt

55. Tavastehus
56. St. Michel
57. Uleaborg
58. Viborg

Poland:

59. Kalish
60. Kieltse
61. Lomzha
62. Liublin
63. Petrokov

64. Radom
65. Siedlitz
66. Suvalki
67. Warsaw

North Caucasus Region:

68. Baku
69. Derbent
70. Ekaterinodar (Kuban)
71. Elisavetpul or Elisavetpol
72. Erivan

73. Kars
74. Kutais or Batum
75. Stavropol
76. Tiflis
77. Vladtkavkas (Terek)

Note: The Yaroslav region is not named on Map A. It is number 50 on Map B.

Note: The towns of Odessa and Volgograd, formerly Stalingrad, are not on the maps in IR. I added those to my maps because of their historical importance. Stalingrad was called Tsaritsyn before about 1925.

Map A

Map B

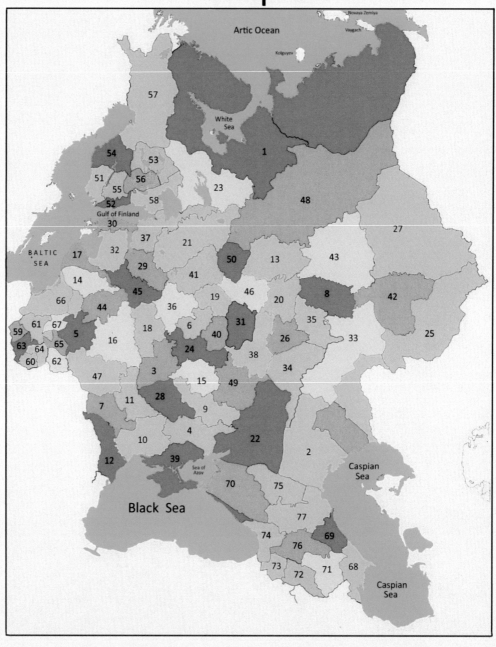

Introduction

Highlights:

Russia is a massive country sprawling over two continents and across 11 time zones. This book is concerned with the part west of the Ural Mountains which is known as European Russia.

European Russia itself covers a large territory. Tundra is dominant in the far north where moss and lichens feed reindeer which, in turn, support a small population of people. Further south forests interspersed with meadows occur. Here cattle and some crops are raised. The forest land gives way to the steppe or prairie as you continue south. This is the grain growing region of Russia. Then on the southern edge of the Crimean Mountains and the southern Caucasus Mountains, the climate is mild enough to grow crops such as cotton and rice.

The Ural Mountains are low rising to only 6,200 feet above sea level. If you leave out the Crimean and Caucasus Mountains, the rest of European Russia is just a low rolling landscape with maximum elevation of just several hundred feet above sea level and dropping down to about 90 feet below sea level at the Caspian Sea. Because of this mild gradient, the rivers in Russia are slow.

However, the climate and soil vary a great deal. Cold temperatures and poor soil are the rule in the north whereas good soil and moderate or warm temperatures are common in the south.

Despite the large size of and the varied conditions over Russia, some regions do share common physical or climatic features, common economic conditions or common population characteristics. Accordingly, the governments of Russia can be grouped somewhat naturally into the following fourteen regions (the numbers in parentheses correspond to the numbers on Map B):

1. Central Agricultural Region: Kursk (15), Orel (24), Tula (40), Riazan (31), Tambov (38) and Voronezh (49).

Topography: Plains with some hills and gullies.
Soil: Chernoziom and fertile.
Population: 2,400 per square mile.
Arable Land: 70—90%.
Crops: Rye, oats, buckwheat and millet. Also wheat, flax, hemp, sunflowers and tobacco.
Forest Cover: 10—20%.
Livestock: Cattle, horses and sheep.

2. Middle Volga Region: Simbirsk (35), Saratov (34), Penza (26), Kazan (8) and Nizhni-Novgorod (20).

Topography: Varied and undulating.
Soil: Poor north and south but chernoziom in the middle.
Population: Great Russians in the majority. 1,600 per square mile.
Arable Land: 55%.
Crops: Rye, Oats and wheat. Also spelt, buckwheat, millet, sunflower, flax and hemp.
Forest Cover: 12—38% from south to north.
Livestock: Cattle and sheep.

3. Little Russian Region: Kharkov (9), Chernigov (3) and Poltava (28).

Topography: Level in the north; rolling with gullies in the south.
Soil: Sandy in the north and chernoziom over the rest.
Population: Mainly Little Russians. 2,500 per square mile.
Arable Land: 62%.
Crops: Rye, buckwheat, Oats, wheat and barley. Also tobacco and hemp.
Forest Cover: 9—22%.
Livestock: Cattle, horses and sheep.

4. South-Western Region: Volyn (47), Podolsk (7) and Kiev (11).

Topography: Hilly.

Soil: Chernoziom in the middle and lower part.
Population: Mostly Little Russians. 2,600 per square mile.
Arable Land: 50%.
Crops: Sugar beets, rye, winter wheat and oats.
Forest Cover: 25—32%.
Livestock: Cattle, horses and sheep.

5. Novorossisk Region: Bessarabia (12), Kherson (10), Taurida (39), Don (22) and Ekaterinoslav (4).

Topography: Steppe. Hilly between Dniester and Prut.
Soil: Chernoziom.
Population: Great Russians predominate. 1,300 per square mile.
Arable Land: 46%.
Crops: Spring wheat, maize, rye and barley. Also flax, tobacco and vines.
Forest Cover: 3%.
Livestock: Cattle, sheep and horses. Also camels in the southeast.

6. Lower Volga Region: Samara (33), Orenburg (25) and Astrakhan (2).

Topography: Varied from mountainous in the northeast to plains below sea level near the Caspian Sea.
Soil: Chernoziom in the north to salt marshes and sand in the south.
Population: 470 per square mile.
Arable Land: 9—38%.
Crops: Spring wheat, rye, millet and oats.
Forest Cover: 12%.
Livestock: Cattle, horses, sheep and camels.

7. Moscow Industrial Region: Vladimir (46), Moscow (19), Kaluga (6), Tver (41), Yaroslav (50) and Kostroma (13).

Topography: Some level land and some hilly land.
Soil: Not much fertile soil.

Population: 1,700 to 3,500 per square mile.
Arable Land: Less than 30%.
Crops: Rye, oats and barley. Also potatoes and flax for fiber.
Forest Cover: 42—60%.
Livestock: Cattle, horses and some sheep.

8. White Russian Region: Moghilev (18), Minsk (16), Vitebsk (45) and Smolensk (36).

Topography: Rolling hills, swamps and bogs.
Soil: Poor.
Population: 1,260 per square mile mainly White Russians.
Arable Land: 27%.
Crops: Rye, oats, barley and buckwheat. Also potatoes and flax for fiber.
Forest Cover: 37%.
Livestock: Cattle, horses and sheep.

9. Lithuanian Region: Kovno (14), Vilno (44) and Grodno (5).

Topography: Hilly and forested.
Soil: Not fertile.
Population: Lithuanians at about 1,800 per square mile.
Arable Land: 40%.
Crops: Potatoes, rye, oats and barley. Also flax for fiber.
Forest Cover: 25%.
Livestock: Cattle, sheep and horses.

10. Vistula Region: Suvalk (66), Lomzha (61), Plotsk (see Remarks). Siedlets (65), Lublin (62), Warsaw (67), Radom (64), Kielets (60), Petrokov (63) and Kalish (59).

Topography: Mountainous in the south and level with swamps in the north.
Soil: Clay and somewhat fertile.
Population: Polish people at about 3,600 per square mile.

Arable Land: No information given.
Crops: Rye, oats, potatoes, flax, winter wheat and sugar beets.
Forest Cover: 25%.
Livestock: No information given.

11. Baltic Region: Lithuania (32), Courland (17) and Esthonia (30).

Topography: Undulating plains.
Soil: Clay and sand.
Population: Lettish and Finnish people at about 1,370 per square mile.
Arable Land: 20—30%.
Crops: Rye, barley and oats. Also potatoes and flax.
Forest Cover: 26%.
Livestock: Cattle, horses and sheep.

12. Lake Region: Olonets (23), Novgorod (21), St. Petersburg (37) and Pskov (29).

Topography: Hilly in the west and swamps and river valleys in the east.
Soil: Poor.
Population: 700 per square mile.
Arable Land: 10% overall but up to 27% in Pskov.
Crops: Rye, oats, barley and flax.
Forest Cover: 52%.
Livestock: Cattle, horses and sheep.

13. Extreme North Region: Vologda (48) and Archangel (1).

Topography: Mostly level.
Soil: No information given.
Population: 50 per square mile.
Arable Land: 1%.
Crops: Barley, rye and oats. Also flax and potatoes.
Forest Cover: 60—86%.
Livestock: Cattle, horses and sheep.

14. Ural Region: Viatka (43), Perm (27) and Ufa (42).

Topography: Varied and approaching the Ural Mountains.
Soil: Clay in the north and chernoziom in the south.
Population: Mostly Great Russians at 700 per square mile.
Arable Land: 10—31%.
Crops: Rye and oats. Also spring wheat, barley, spelt and flax.
Forest Cover: 62%.
Livestock: Horses, cattle and sheep.

Remarks:

A) Voronezh is spelled Voronesh and Moghilev is spelled Mogilev on Map A.

B) Chernoziom will be defined in Chapter II.

C) Little Russians is a name that was used for Ukrainians.

D) Novorossisk translates to "New Russia."

E) White Russians is an outdated term used to denote the people living in present-day Belarus and Great Russians was used to describe the people living in central and northern European Russia.

F) Map A has only nine names for the Vistula region but the introduction of IR gives ten names including Plotsk. Plotsk is not on the map and hence not on our base map or in List A. Plotsk is probably Polotsk, Belarus. Kielets (Kielce) is spelled Kieltse on Map A.

G) The governments represented by Reval, Riga and Mitau correspond (roughly) to present-day Estonia, Latvia and Lithuania, respectively.

Chapter I. The Climate.

Highlights

Due to the vastness of Russia, there is wide variation in the climate of its various regions. But the differences over European Russia, especially if the far north is excluded, are not as extreme. In a table on page 3 of IR, the lowest average January temperature for stations of latitude 60 degrees or less is -15.3 C in Orenburg which is in the eastern part. The maximum average temperature for July is 29 C for Baku which is on the shores of the Caspian Sea. More centrally located cities and their average January and July temperatures in degrees Celsius and Fahrenheit are:

Location	January Average (C/F)	July Average (C/F)
Kiev	-6.1/21.0	19.3/66.7
Odessa	-3.6/25.5	22.6/72.7
Simferopol	-0.6/30.9	20.7/69.3
Moscow	-11.0/12.2	18.9/66.0

The altitude above sea level also does not vary much over European Russia. For the stations in the table on page 3 of IR, leaving out stations in the Caucasus and Crimean mountains, the maximum elevation is 254 meters (833 feet) at Simferopol which is at the foot of Crimean Mountains. The minimum elevation is -20 meters (-66.6 feet) at Astrakhan which at the mouth of the Volga River where it empties into the Caspian Sea.

Additional tables in Chapter I give the average number of days field work can be done at the various reporting stations as well as the average number of growing days, the average harvest date, the yearly precipitation and the precipitation during the crucial months of May to September. Generally speaking the northeastern parts of Russia are colder and wetter than the southwestern areas. The most drought prone areas are along the Black Sea and northwest of the Caspian Sea. While western winds are the rule in the summer in southern Russia, very dry, warm winds from the east are also common and dry out crops.

Here are some data from the Table "Rainfall in Inches" on page 7 of IR.

City	Yearly Rainfall in Inches	Rainfall (May-September)
Moscow	21.1	11.5
Kiev	20.5	11.1
Chernigov	18.0	10.6
Odessa	15.7	8.1
Saratov	17.6	8.3
Novotcherkassk	17.5	9.0

The black-earth region (which will be defined later) of Russia has similar temperatures as the prairie region of the US. However, the US regions get more precipitation than the Russian areas. And the rains in the US are more widespread whereas the moisture in Russia is more likely to come in the form of isolated thunderstorms.

Remarks:

The first two maps in this chapter (Chapter I. Climate, Map No. 1a and Chapter I. Climate, Map No. 1b) show isothermal lines for January and July. These maps are based on the map opposite page 4 in IR.

The temperatures on Maps 1a and 1b are given in degrees Fahrenheit. If you want to convert to degrees Celsius, subtract 32 from the Fahrenheit number, multiply the result by 5 and then divide by 9. Here is a small table of equivalent temperatures:

F°	C°
32	0
50	10
68	20
77	25
86	30

The third map in this chapter (Chapter I. Climate, Map No. 2) gives lines of atmospheric precipitation. Note the dry areas in northwest Crimea and above the Caspian Sea.

JANUARY ISOTHERMAL LINES IN DEGREES FAHRENHEIT.

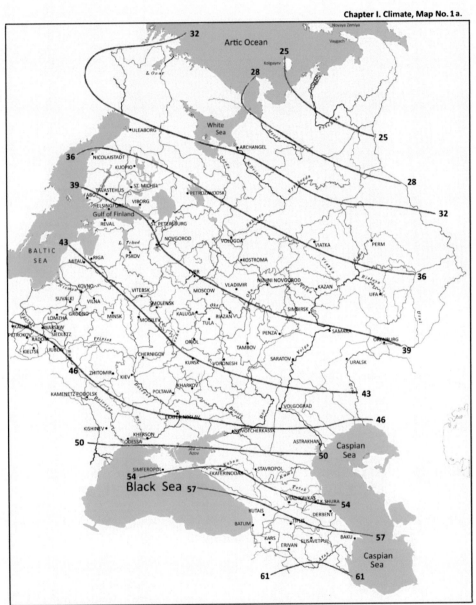

Based on the work by A. Voieikov and cartographical work by A Jlyne S.P.B.

JULY ISOTHERMAL LINES IN DEGREES FAHRENHEIT

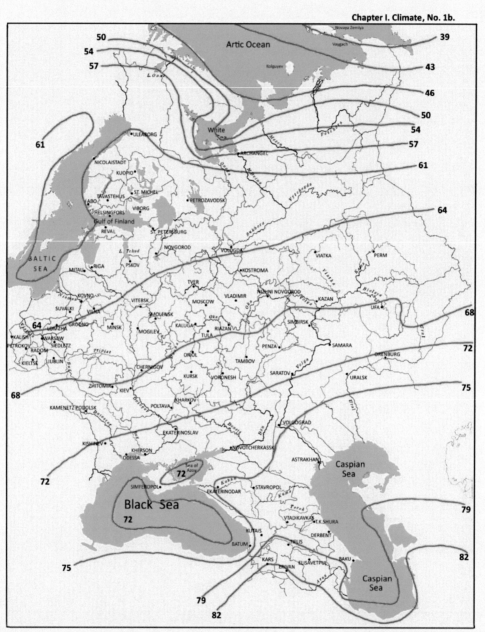

Based on the work of A. Voieikov and cartographical works of A. Jlyne S.P.B.

MAP OF ATMOSPHERIC PRECIPITATION

Chapter I. Climate, Map No. 2.

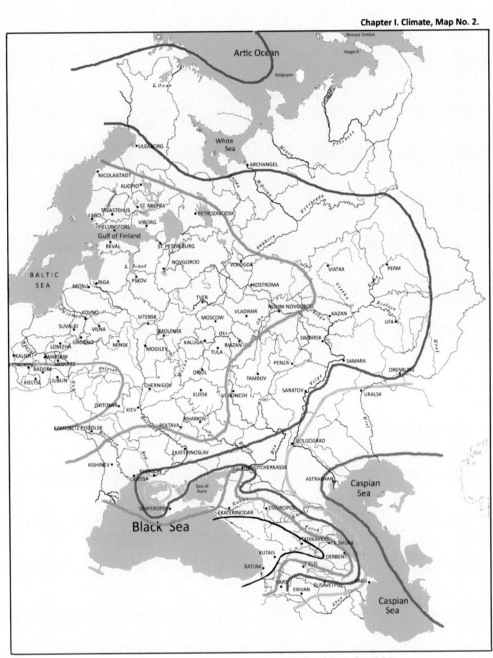

Based on the work of A. Voieikov and cartographical work by A. Jlyne S.P.B.

Annual precipitation in millimeters and inches.

200 / 7.87

300 / 11.81

400 / 15.75

500 / 19.69

600 / 23.61

800 / 31.5

Chapter II. The Soil.

Highlights:

European Russia can be divided into two parts on the basis of its soil. The area to the southeast of the line shown on Map A is the "black earth" or chernoziom (chernozom) area of Russia. To the northeast of that line are the non-chernoziom soil types which underlie the more forested part of the country. Chernoziom is very high in humus and nitrogen and makes the soil remarkably fertile (IR, 26). There is a lot of overlap between the steppes of Russia and the chernoziom region.

Remarks:

The dark curve or line on Map A is part of many maps in IR. To avoid clutter, we have chosen to show it on that base map only. Subtypes of chernoziom are shown on Chapter II. Soil, Map No. 1.

The vast majority of German colonies were situated below the demarcation line shown on Map A. Hence it is correct to say that German colonists had rich, black soil to farm.

The rest of IR Chapter II consists of a detailed chemical analysis of the soils of European Russia.

From now on, we will reference pages in IR with just a number within parentheses.

Map No. 5 in Chapter III is related to the information in this chapter and to Map No. 1 in this chapter.

Chapters II and V have only one map each. Nevertheless they label the maps as Map No. 1 in those chapters. We follow their custom on this for historical reasons.

MAP OF THE PRINCIPAL SOILS OF THE CHERNOZIOM REGION.

Chapter II. Soil, Map No. 1.

Artic Ocean

Novaya Zemlya
Vaygach

Kolguyev

White Sea

ULEABORG

ARCHANGEL

NICOLAISTADT

KUOPIO

ST. MICHEL

TAVASTEHUS
ABO
HELSINGFORS
Gulf of Finland
REVAL

PETROZAVODSK

VIBORG

ST. PETERSBURG

NOVGOROD

VOLOGDA

VIATKA

PERM

BALTIC SEA

MITAU
RIGA
PSKOV

L. Tchud

TVER

KOSTROMA

NIZHNI NOVGOROD

UFA

KOVNO

VITEBSK

MOSCOW

VLADIMIR

KAZAN

SUVALKI
VILNA

SMOLENSK

MINSK

MOGILEV

KALUGA

TULA

RIAZAN

SIMBIRSK

SAMARA

ORENBURG

KALISH
WARSAW
PETROKOV
RADOM
SIEDLETZ
KIELTSE
LIUBLIN

Pripiat

CHERNIGOV

ORIOL

TAMBOV

PENZA

SARATOV

URALSK

ZHITOMIR
KIEV

KURSK

VORONESH

KAMENETZ PODOLSK

KHARKOV

POLTAVA

EKATERINOSLAV

KISHINEV

NOVOTCHERKASSK

VOLGOGRAD

ASTRAKHAN

KHERSON
ODESSA

Sea of Azov

Caspian Sea

SIMFEROPOL

EKATERINODAR

STAVROPOL

Black Sea

VTADIKAVKAS
T.K. SHURA

KUTAIS

DERBENT

BATUM

TIFLIS

BAKU

KARS
ERIVAN
ELISAVETPUL

Caspian Sea

Based on the work of P. A. Kostychev and cartographical work by A. Jlyne S.P.B.

| Lime soil | Sand | Grey forest land | Salt marshes dispersed in small areas | Chernoziom |

Chapter III. Rural Population and Landed Property.

Highlights:

In 1885 only about 13% of the population lived in towns. The corresponding figure for the US in 1890 was 29% (42).

(44): "It may not be out of place to mention here, that among the comparatively few emigrants to the United States coming from Russia, the non-Russian element vastly predominates. The bon fide Russians, namely, the Great, Little and White Russians, who are induced to seek their fortune away from their native homes, always prefer to settle on some virgin tract within the confines of their own immense country."

Waste lands are defined to be swamp, barren ground, rocks as well as land used for roads and buildings (44).

In the fifty governments of European Russia, about 26.2% of the land is arable, 15.9% is meadow, 38.8% is forest and 19.1% is waste land.

The Emancipation Act of February 19, 1861 freed the serfs. A majority of serfs received between two and seven dessiatines of land by this act. They had to pay for this land over a number of years (55, 58).

"The Russian people are divided into five clearly defined classes: the nobility, clergy, merchants, burghers and peasants" (45).

Remarks:

This chapter is packed with information and the highlights above only touch on a few of the topics covered. For example, on pages 48–61, the history of serfdom and management of communal lands are discussed in great detail.

The legend of Chapter III. Map No. 1 in IR is based on the number of inhabitants per square kilometer but the numbers on the map itself give the number of inhabitants per square mile. I found this a bit confusing and so I changed the legend to correspond to the numbers on the map.

Several districts in the original map are not colored correctly. For example, Voronezh has 99.6 inhabitants per square English mile according to the map. This number converts to 38.4 inhabitants per square kilometer (see mathematical considerations below). Yet it is colored as belonging to the class with 20–30 inhabitants. The chart and discussion below show that several other governments are colored incorrectly. Some are not as far off as Voronezh but I decided to treat all "discrepancies" as items to be corrected rather than judging which ones are off by enough to be listed as mistakes and which ones are tolerable. My decision was based in part on additional more noticeable mistakes in later maps which I will point out when I discuss those. I hope my criticism is taken as benevolent as I am sure I have added a few mistakes to these pages myself.

Map No. 2 in Chapter III of IR has so much information on it that I decided to break it into two maps for this book (Map No. 2a and Map No. 2b).

Map No. 3 deals with forest cover in European Russia.

Map No. 4 concerns state lands, peasant lands and private lands. Peasant lands include land owned by the serfs freed in 1861 as well as land owned by foreign colonists such as Germans (45). Private land included land owned primarily by nobles and merchants (46–47).

Map No. 5 is related to Map. No. 1 in Chapter II as well as to the chernoziom soil line on Map A in the Preliminaries Chapter.

Mathematical Considerations:

If we use the numbers on the map which are the number of inhabitants per square mile and convert those numbers to the number of inhabitants per square kilometer, we get the following table:

	A	B	C	D
Novotcherkassk	25.7	9.9232	9.9228	10 — 20
Kars	22.7	8.7649	8.7645	10 — 20
Novgorod	25.7	9.9232	9.9228	10 — 20
Voronezh	99.6	38.4573	38.4556	20 — 30
Chernigov	102.5	39.5770	39.5753	40 — 50
Tambov	101.4	39.1523	39.1506	40 — 50
Derbent	53.6	20.6959	20.6950	10 — 20
Tiflis	50.2	19.3831	19.3823	20 — 30
Stavropol	24.8	9.5757	9.5753	10 — 20

Nicolaistadt	25.7	9.9232	9.9228	10 — 20
Yarsolav	76.3	29.4608	29.4595	30 — 40

The numbers in column A come from the original map in IR. The numbers in column B are calculated using the conversion factor 1 ft = 0.304794 meters given on page XIII on IR. The numbers in Column C are calculated using the conversion factor 1 ft = 0.3048006 meters commonly found in English texts. Column D gives the class (and hence the color) for that area. But by either calculation the numbers in columns B and C indicate that Novotcherkassk, Kars, Novgorod, Derbent, Stavropol and Nicolaistadt belong to the class "less than 10" but are colored as belonging to the class 10 — 20.

DENSITY OF POPULATION

Chapter III. Rural population and landed property, Map No. 1.

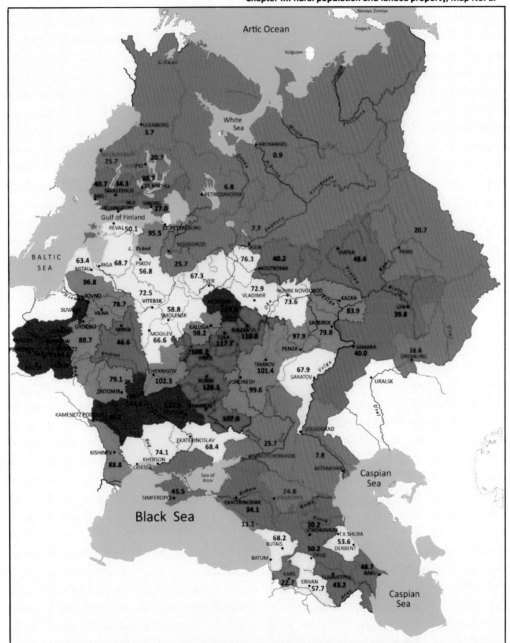

Based on the work of D. Semenov and the cartographical works of Jlyne S.P.B.

Number of inhabitants per square mile.

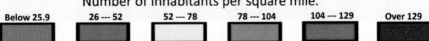

Below 25.9   26 --- 52   52 --- 78   78 --- 104   104 --- 129   Over 129

The figures on the map show the number of inhabitants to 1 square English mile.

AREA OF CULTIVATED LAND IN PERCENTAGE OF THE WHOLE SURFACE FOR EACH GOVERNMENT.

Chapter III. Rural population and landed property, Map No. 2a.

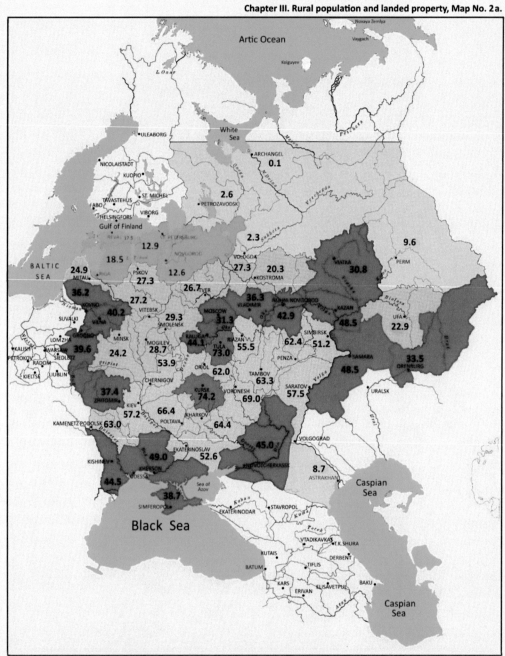

Based on the work by D. Semenov & A. Fortunatov and cartographical works by A. Jlyne S.P.B.

Cultivated or arable lands cover

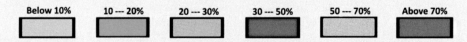

| Below 10% | 10 --- 20% | 20 --- 30% | 30 --- 50% | 50 --- 70% | Above 70% |

The figures on the map show the area of cultivated lands in percentage of the whole surface of each government.

AREA OF CULTIVATED LAND IN PERCENTAGE OF THE WHOLE SURFACE FOR EACH GOVERNMENT.

Chapter III. Rural population and landed property, Map No. 2b.

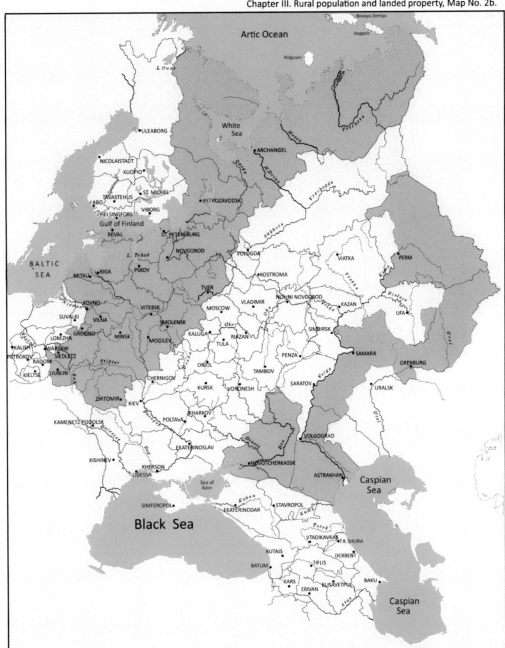

Based on the work of D. Semenov & A. Fortunatov and cartographical work by A. Jlyne S.P.B.

The orange areas are the governments with waste land covering over 10% of the surface.

PROPORTION OF FOREST IN PERCENTAGE OF THE WHOLE SURFACE ACCORDING TO GOVERNMENTS.

Chapter III. Rural population and landed property, Map No. 3.

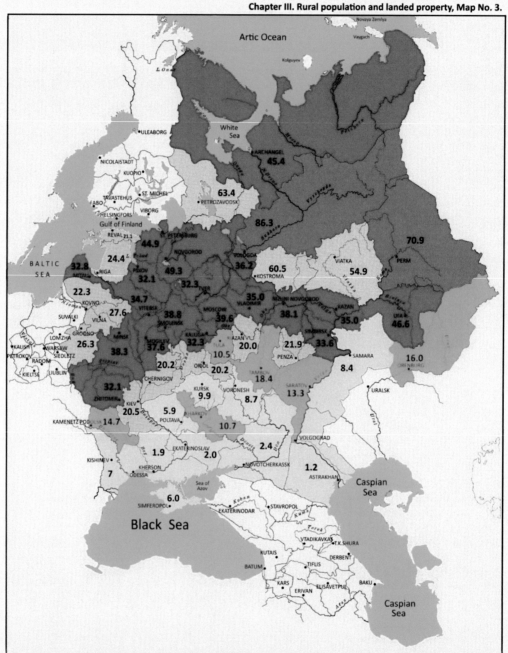

Based on work by D. Semenov and cartographical works by A. Jlyne S.P.B.

Forests cover.

| Below 10% | 10 --- 20% | 20 --- 30% | 30 --- 50% | 50 --- 70% | Above 70% |

The figures on the map show forest area in percentage of the whole surface.

OWNERSHIP OF LAND.

Chapter III. Rural population and landed property. Map No. 4.

Artic Ocean

Novaya Zemlya

Vaygach

Kolguyev

White
Sea

ARCHANGEL

• ULEABORG

NICOLAISTADT •

KUOPIO •

• PETROZAVODSK

TAVASTEHUS • ST. MICHEL

ABO
HELSINGFORS • VIBORG

Gulf of Finland

REVAL •

ST. PETERSBURG

VOLOGDA
NOVGOROD

VIATKA

PERM •

BALTIC
SEA

MITAU • • RIGA

PSKOV

KOSTROMA
• KOSTROMA

TVER •

NIZHNI NOVGOROD

KAZAN

KOVNO •

VITEBSK •

MOSCOW

VLADIMIR

UFA •

SUVALKI •

VILNA •

SMOLENSK

OKA

SIMBIRSK

GRODNO •

MINSK •

MOGILEV •

KALUGA •

RIAZAN

LOMZHA

TULA •

PENZA

SAMARA •

KALISH

WARSAW
SIEDLETZ

ORIOL •

TAMBOV •

ORENBURG •

PETROKOV •
RADOM •

CHERNIGOV •

KURSK •

VORONESH •

SARATOV •

URALSK •

KIELTSE •
LIUBLIN •

ZHITOMIR •

KIEV •

KHARKOV •

POLTAVA •

KAMENETZ PODOLSK •

EKATERINOSLAV •

VOLGOGRAD •

KISHINEV •

KHERSON •
ODESSA •

NOVOTCHERKASSK •

ASTRAKHAN •

Caspian
Sea

SIMFEROPOL •

Sea of
Azov

Kuban

STAVROPOL •
EKATERINODAR •

Black Sea

Terek

VTADIKAVKAS • T.K.SHURA

KUTAIS •

DERBENT •

BATUM •

TIFLIS •

KARS •

ELISAVETPUL •

BAKU •

ERIVAN •

Caspian
Sea

Based on the work of A. Fortunatov and the cartographical works of Jlyne S.P.B.

Governments with State lands covering more than one-half of the surface.

Governments with Peasant lands covering more than one-half of the surface.

Governments with Private lands covering more than one-half of the surface.

DISTRIBUTION OF DIFFERENT KINDS OF LAND.

Chapter III. Rural population and landed property, Map No. 5.

Based on work by A. Fortunatov and cartographical work by A. Jlyne S.P.B.

Distribution of the prevailing kinds of land.

⬜	Field, Meadow, Forest	⬛	Meadow, Forest, Field
⬜	Field, Forest, Meadow	⬜	Forest, Meadow, Field
⬜	Meadow, Field, Forest	⬛	Forest, Field, Meadow

*Steppes are counted under meadow.

Chapter IV. Systems of Agriculture and Field-Rotation.

Highlights:

Climate, soil, density of population, land ownership, means of communication and transport have all played a role in the development of agriculture in Russia.

Most Russians make a living by farming but there are exceptions. In the far north, forestry, fishing, hunting and making tar sustain a small population. And in the lower parts of the Don and Volga as well as in the northern Caucasus, cattle raising is the chief industry.

Flax for fiber is raised primarily in the Governments of Pskov, Vitebsk, Novgorod and parts of Yaroslav, Kostroma, Smolensk, Vologda, Tver and Curland (65). (See Map 1 in Chapter VIII).

Cattle and the dairy industry are prevalent in the Governments of St. Petersburg, Livland, Estland, Curland, Kovno, Grodno, Vilna, Mogilev, Moscow, Kaluga and in parts of Smolensk, Tver, Yaroslav, Kostroma, Vladimir, Riazan and Tula as well as in some other governments (66). (See Maps 1, 2 and 4 in Chapter X).

Grain production based on the three-year alternation system is common in the Governments of Tula, Riazan, Tambov, Penza, Simbirsk, Nizhni-Novgorod, Kazan, Orel, Kursk, Chernigov and parts of Saratov, Voronezh, Kharkov, Poltava, Kiev, Podolsk and Volyn. Winter wheat, rye, spring wheat, oats and buckwheat are raised in these governments (66). (See the Maps in Chapter VI and the Diagrams in Chapters VI and VII).

Grain production based on the many-year alternation system is found in the Governments of Saratov, Samara, Voronezh, Kharkov, Poltava, Ekaterinoslav and Kherson. Cattle and sheep raising is also prominent in this area. Crops grown here include wheat, millet, oats, barley and peas (66). (See the Maps in Chapter VI and the Diagrams in Chapters VI and VII).

Beets are grown in the Governments of Tula, Tambov, Voronezh, Samara, Kursk, Kharkov, Chernigov, Kiev, Podolsk and Volynia (67).

Different kinds of tobacco are grown in various localities including the Governments of Poltava, Chernigov, Kharkov, Kursk, Orel, Bessarabia, Tauride, Samara, Tula, Riazan, Simbirsk, Penza, Tambov, Voronezh as well as in Caucasus regions (67).

Crop rotation schemes are common including giving land a "rest" for ten to fifteen years (69).

Remarks:

A variety of crop rotation schemes are shown on pages 69–72 in IR.

In this chapter, Courland is spelled Curland and Eastland is spelled Estland.

Chapter V. Cultivation of the Soil.

Highlights:

Fertilizing:

The primary fertilizer used in Russia is animal manure.

"Still farther to the south follows a strip of land, where the fertilizing of fields began not more than eight years ago. The peasants of this region do not manure their fields in the least, excepting the German colonists there found" (76).

Remark: I believe they are referring to the lands below the light blue colored area on Map No. 1 of this chapter.

". . . in some place of Kherson and Tauride, also in the districts of Tsaritzyn and Kamyshin of the governments of Saratov, and in Novouzensk and Nicolaev of the government of Samara, fertilizers are used neither in the farming of proprietors nor of peasants. Several very intelligent proprietors of these regions not only do not manure their fields but even claim that such fertilizing is injurious, arguing that manured fields suffer far more from drought than those unmanured" (77).

Tobacco and hemp fields are the most heavily manured.

Hauling manure some distance is too costly and so manuring is done most heavily near cattle yards.

The season for manuring varies widely over European Russia and for different crops. Manure is sometimes mixed with straw, peat, moss, leafs and so on.

Some artificial phosphates are used in some areas.

Plowing:

In the north, with some exceptions in the Polish and Baltic areas, the soil is generally plowed with the Russian **sokha** hitched to one horse. A less primitive plow is called a **kosila.** With the sokha, the soil is generally plowed to a depth of 1.5 to 2.5 vershocks (a vershock is 7/4 of an inch).

In the southern and eastern steppe regions, the soil is so hard to work that the Russian sokha is useless. Here a two-wheeled plow, the Little Russian saban, is used. Regarding the sokha and saban, the authors write (82): "By means of such a patriarchal instrument the ploughing of all the Russian steppes is effected, and only in later years has the many-knived plough been introduced, invented and constructed in the German colonies of southern Russia."

This new "many-knived plough" is called a boukker (264).

"In many estates . . . the cultivation of the soil is effected, if possible at least once a year, with more or less improved ploughs, generally that of the German Hohenheim or the sack type being used in this region. For harrowing the soil, iron harrows or wooden with iron teeth are employed. Many farmers have cultivators for softening the soil, and for successful farming, ploughs with many points, mostly of German type. In many estates of the non-steppe Chernoziom region, drills and sowers are used" (91).

Sowing:

Sowing methods vary from crop to crop and region to region. After plowing, the fields may be harrowed with wooden harrows fitted with iron teeth. Then the fields are sown by hand and covered by another plowing and harrowing.

Seed is sown most thickly on the non-chernoziom lands. Less is sown in chernoziom non-steppe regions and the least amount of seed per given area is sown on the black-earth soil of the steppes.

Wheat is generally sown by hand but on large estates drills are sometimes used.

In the southern steppes, the late spring is quickly followed by a hot and often dry summer. So seeding must be done at the earliest possible moment.

Reaping:

Reaping begins with the use of a sickle or scythe. Small sheaves are collected into shocks. If possible, once these shocks are dry, they are hauled to and stored in a barn. Threshing is done by hand with the use of a flail or by the garman method (see below).

Machines have gradually replaced hand-methods in the raising of grain. The next quotes give us some information about this transformation.

"Until very recently the reaping of wheat and of other cereals was by hand, while now the hand-reaper is largely supplanted by machines. For this purpose the majority of even the smallest peasant farmers provide themselves with reaping machines built on the steppe region and sold for comparatively small prices. These instruments are mostly of very imperfect construction; they have no binding apparatus and even no contrivance for throwing off the sheaves, that work being done by a workman sitting on the machine. Grain thus reaped and thrown on the field is not tied into sheaves but is laid in ricks like hay, and remains so until removed from the field, the hauling being done only after the reaping completed, generally in the latter part of August. These ricks are hauled to the thrashing-places, which are generally on the farms. The vastness of the fields and their usually great distance from the farmhouses cause the removal of the crops to be one of the most difficult tasks of the farmer" (84).

Threshing:

The following quote about the threshing of flax is representative and descriptive of the process used to thresh grains.

"The thrashing is done generally in a very primitive way, notwithstanding the high value of the seed. For this a special open place or thrashing-bed, called tock, is prepared on sufficiently hard meadow land, and which is mown very closely and duly cleared, where the thrashing is done with the garman. For this purpose the flax is laid on the thrashing-floor, in the form of a large ring, over which horses are driven, first at a slow pace, and after the mass has grown more compact, at a trot; the crumpled and crushed flax is then turned, and again horses are driven over it as before until all the kernels have been set free. The entire mass is then shaken out with rakes; the straw is removed, and the thrashed grain is shoveled in the centre of the thrashing-floor. However, flax is not everywhere thrashed by means of this method; in many places instead, horses with carts filled by men are driven over the flax-floors, and as many as possible. The thrashing by means of carts goes more rapidly than by horses only. In other places stone-rollers are used instead of carts for this purpose. After the thrashing is finished, the cleaning is begun on the thrashing-place by hand-methods, with the aid of the spade and the wind. If the crops are abundant the winnowing continues the whole autumn. In some places, however, there are cleaning machines, mostly hand implements, with which the work goes more rapidly. After winnowing, the grain is further cleaned by large hand sieves, but even by means of sifting, the grain cannot be perfectly cleaned" (83–84).

"The thrashing of wheat and of other cereals is effected in different ways; on the estates of the rich proprietors it is by means of improved complicated steam-machines, very much used in the south; on the majority of large, and in many of the smaller estates of the peasants and colonists, horse thrashing machines are used; while in a few places thrashing is done with the flail or by the garman method. The threshed grain is best cleaned by hand fanning-mills and assorting machines; in some cases the work is done by means of hand-sieves. The grain of the southern steppe region contains a greater or less percentage of impurities according to the methods in use for cleaning" (84–85).

Some custom threshing is done by groups of peasants who collectively purchase horse-powered machines for this purpose.

"As to the natural qualities of the grain the special red wheat of that region [steppe region] excels all others; the kernel is plump and dry, has a thin hull and gives a large proportion of white flour and of nitrogen, and has well deserved its reputation on the European markets" (85).

Other crops:

Watermelons, muskmelons, cucumbers, pumpkins and squashes are grown in eastern parts of European Russia.

Remarks:

Sowing rates for various grains are given in meras per dessiatine on pages 74–75 or IR. A Russian mera is the same as a chetverik (cetverik) and is equivalent to 0.7446 US bushels according to the website

http://www.convert-me.com/en/convert/history_volume/cetverik.html

A dessiatine is 2.6697 acres. So to convert meras per dessiatine to bushels per acre multiply by 0.7446 and divide by 2.6697. The table below gives the sowing rates they used in meras per dessiatine and the equivalent in bushels per acre.

Sowing Rates:

	Meras per dessiatine		Bushels per acre	
Crop	Low	High	Low	High
Rye	4.5	12	1.3	3.3
Winter Wheat	4	12	1.1	3.3
Spring Wheat	4	12	1.1	3.3
Oats	6	24	1.7	6.7
Barley	4	18	1.1	5.0
Buckwheat	3	14	0.8	3.9
Millet	1	2.5	0.3	0.7
Indian Corn	1	2.5	0.3	0.7
Spelt	6	16	1.7	4.5
Peas	3	12	0.8	3.3
Potatoes	10	240	2.8	66.9

Sowing rates depend a great deal on the amount of available moisture. This may explain, in part, why the sowing rates were least in the chernoziom steppe regions.

The many-knived plow they describe is a multi-shared plow or a multi-bottom plow. It was called a boukker by the Russians (264). It is also described at the site http://gameo.org/index.php?title=Farm_machinery where it is called a bukker.

See also Chapter XII of this book.

The reaping machine discussed in the text is the Hussey Reaper, a picture of which can be seen at https://en.wikipedia.org/wiki/Reaper or in Bosch, page 61.

A "rick" is a rectangular pile of hay or cut grain.

They use the word "thrashing" to describe the process of removing kernels of grain from cut plants. I prefer threshing.

Map No. 1 is the only map in this chapter.

46

FERTILIZING.

Chapter V. Cultivation of the soil, Map No. 1.

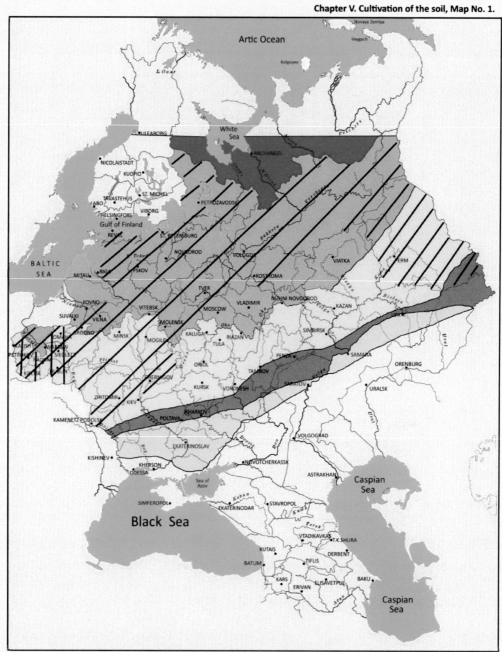

Based on the work of D. Semenov and cartographical work of A. Jlyne S.P.B.

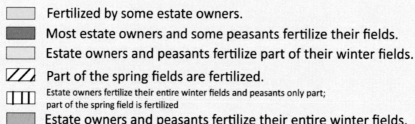

Fertilized by some estate owners.

Most estate owners and some peasants fertilize their fields.

Estate owners and peasants fertilize part of their winter fields.

Part of the spring fields are fertilized.

Estate owners fertilize their entire winter fields and peasants only part;
part of the spring field is fertilized

Estate owners and peasants fertilize their entire winter fields.

Entire winter and spring fields are fertilized.

Chapter VI. Breadstuffs.

Highlights:

In general about 60% –70% of arable land is sown annually in European Russia. The rest is fallow. The far north, the Baltic provinces and the southern and south-eastern regions are exceptions. In Orenburg, as little as 30% of the arable land is planted each year.

Rye is sown on more land than any other crop in European Russia. Next, in order, are oats, wheat, barley, buckwheat and millet. Potatoes, maize, spelt, peas, beets, tobacco, flax, hemp, rape, sunflowers, poppy and mustard are also grown.

More information about those lesser crops appears in Chapter VIII and on the Maps 1 and 2 in that chapter.

There is little difference between the percentage of acreage devoted to the different crops by peasants and by landowners. The only notable exception is the percentage of spring wheat with landowners at 21% and peasants at 14.9% (94).

Peasants sow 72.3% of the total land sown and landowners sow the other 27.6% (94).

The percentage of cultivated land planted with each of the major crops is shown on Maps 1–8 of this chapter. Map 9 gives a composite picture of the prevailing crops. The percentages in Maps 1–8 are of the land sown not of all the arable land. And these figures are based on the 10–12 years prior to 1892.

Novorossisk can be translated as "new Russia" and refers to the southern steppe governments of Bessarabia, Kherson, Tauride, Ekaterinoslav and Novotcherkassk (Don Region). In this area little oats is sown and wheat is king. Map 2 shows the proportion of wheat that is spring wheat and winter wheat.

The yield per dessiatine is lower in the steppe area than in the non-chernoziom areas. However, the return per amount of seed sown is equal to or greater in the steppe region than in the other areas.

"It is sufficient to note that in the steppe zone the quantity of seed sown of the chief cereals for a given area is only half as great as in the non-steppe localities, and accordingly the yield per dessiatine in the steppe region proves much lower than in the non-Chernoziom districts" (96).

"This difference in the harvests between the Chernoziom and non-Chernoziom governments and in the general the considerable range of the yield in Russia compared with other countries, is chiefly explained by the conditions of the climate and by the primitive methods of farming in the Chernoziom governments. With their natural fertility of soil and limited use of manures, especially in the steppe zone, the climate is of decisive importance. The difference between the Chernoziom and non-Chernoziom zones in respect to poor crops is explained by the fact that droughts are exceedingly frequent and severe in the former, while in the latter they are very rare and never extreme, and by the fact that in the non-Chernoziom governments the dressing of the fields with manure is universal, while in the Chernoziom zone the fields are manured only in the non-steppe regions, and even there to a much less degree. The importance of this fact is evident on considering that the variations in yield in the non-steppe Chernoziom governments are smaller than in the steppe region where manuring of the fields is almost unknown" (100).

"Droughts are not the only causes of bad harvests. In consequence of the severity of the climate of European Russia the winter crops, when there is a lack of snow, sometimes freeze out. Further the crops are often injured by late spring and early autumn frosts. However, as proved by the slight variation of the harvests in the extreme north of Russia and by their enormous fluctuations in the south, the chief climatic agent in harvest is the sufficient or insufficient quantity of atmospheric moisture. A more minute investigation of the influence of the weather upon vegetation shows that in the majority of Chernoziom governments often two or three abundant showers falling at the right time may assure a plentiful yield of the principal crops, while an absence of rain at critical moments, for example during the filling of the grain, is the cause of a more or less considerable failure" (100).

Average yields for rye, spring wheat, oats and potatoes are illustrated in Maps 10–13. Average yields are just part of the story of grain production. Variations in the harvest are another part. That aspect is illustrated in Map 14, in Diagrams 1a and 1b and in the table below which shows the fluctuations from 1883 through 1891 and which appears on page 99 of IR (the numbers are percents of the mean harvest):

Year	Rye	Wheat	Oats	All Sorts
1883	79.6	87.5	100.1	90.7
1884	102.9	106.7	93.4	97.7
1885	105.2	71.1	72.5	82.4
1886	98.1	65.1	104.5	96.2
1887	110.6	113.4	108.7	109.9
1888	111.1	125.4	99.8	110.7
1889	83.9	81.4	91.8	84.1
1890	95.1	85.1	95.6	95.2
1891	70.4	67.1	75.3	73.6

Note that the largest fluctuations occur with the wheat harvest. Also note that 1885 and 1886 were disastrous years for wheat followed by two bumper crops in 1887 and 1888 and then three years of very poor harvests of wheat.

The United States produces and exports more corn and wheat than Russia. However, Russia produces and exports more rye, barley and buckwheat.

The last pages (105–110) of this chapter in IR give information on the varieties of the main cereals along with their growing and milling properties.

Remarks:

Recall that in Chapter V it was pointed out that sowing rates were lower in the richer soils of the chernoziom region than in the non-chernoziom areas. We also quoted from IR that putting manure or other fertilizer on fields may do more harm than good during a drought. This may not be true with present drought-resistant varieties of grain. If we put all this information together and take into account the low precipitation rates for southern Russia, low sowing rates make sense.

The rich soils of the chernoziom area should be sown at a low rate because thick seeding on fertile or fertilized soil and little moisture will lead to a poor or completely failed harvest. In other words, by sowing the rich chernoziom lightly, the farmers tried to maximize the yield in low-moisture years rather than in high-moisture years.

The average yields in Maps 10–13 should not be compared to the current yields in the United States. If you want to make comparisons with yields in this country you should do so for a comparable time period. A yield map for spring wheat for 1890 is available at http://www.loc.gov/resource/g3701gm.gct00010/?sp=98.

We now make comments about some of the maps and diagrams in Chapter VI of IR and the corresponding maps and diagrams in this book.

Map 3: Area under Oats in Percentage of the Whole Cultivated Surface.

On the original map in IR, the government of Mogilev was colored for the class 20–30% but labeled with the percentage 19.2. So I changed the color to correspond to the 10–20% class.

Map 4: Area under Barley in Percentage of the Whole Cultivated Surface.

In the original map in IR, Yaroslav (the district NE of Tver) is labeled 4.0 but colored as if it was in the 5 to 10% range. I assumed the 4.0 number was correct and colored it as belonging to the 1 to 5% range.

The province of Vitebsk is labeled as 14.9 but is colored as in the 15 to 20% range. I changed the color to match the 10-15% range.

Map 10: Average Yield of Rye.

Maps 10 and 11 give the yields in tchetverts (chetverts) per dessiatine as well as in bushels per acre. Maps 12 and 13 give the yields in tchetverts per dessiatine only. I give the yields on all four of these maps in bushels per acre only. There are two reasons for this: first, it reduces the clutter on the maps and, second, tchetverts and dessiatines are no longer used anywhere. To convert tchetverts per dessiatine to bushels per acre, multiply by 2.208225 (5.96/2.699).

Russia is now on the metric system as are most other countries with the exception of the United States and a few small countries. In the metric system, crop yields are commonly stated in tonnes per acre.

A tonne is defined to be 1000 kilograms (one megagram) which is equivalent to 2204.6 pounds. A hectare is an area 100 meters by 100 meters. It is equal to about 2.47 acres (more precisely 2.47105381 acres).

To convert from bushels per acre to tonnes per hectare, we take the weight of a bushel of grain and multiply by the number of bushels and by 2.47 to get the pounds per hectare. We divide this result by 2204.6 to obtain the final result in tonnes per hectare.

For example, 60 bushels of wheat (wheat weighs 60 pounds per bushel) per acre equals 3600 pounds per acre. Multiplying this 3600 by 2.47 and dividing by 2204.6 gives us 4.03 tonnes per hectare.

Some other crops with their weight per bushel are rye (56), barley (48), flax (60), oats (32 in the US but 34 in Canada), shelled corn (56) and potatoes (60).

Additional information about converting from one set of units to another can be found at the following and similar websites:

https://www.extension.iastate.edu/agdm/wholefarm/html/c6-80.html
http://www.agrimoney.com/calculator/grain/

Map 12: Average Yield of Oats.

There seem to be a lot of mismatches between numbers and colors on this map in IR. For example, Penza is labeled as 7.2 (tchetverts per dessiatine) but colored as belonging to the interval 6.5–7. So I assumed the number was correct, not the color, and colored it accordingly (after converting to bushels per acre). The same is true for Riazan, Vladimir, Tver, Archangel, Tula, Poltava and Perm.

Map 13: Average Yield of Potatoes.

The original map gives no number for Moscow.

Map 14: Yearly Deviation in Percentage of the Mean Yield of Rye for a Period of 11 years [1881–1891].

In my copy of IR, this map is labeled Map No. 12. Since it comes between Map 13 and Map 15 and is the second No. 12, I renumbered it to No. 14.

The stacked numbers for each government should be interpreted as follows: The top number is the spread from the lowest deviation from the mean to the highest deviation from the mean. The lower number is the maximal deviation from the mean regardless whether it is positive or negative. For example for Saratov, reading from Diagram No. 1 of this chapter, the maximum yield recorded was approximately 50% over the mean. The minimum yield was approximately -51% below the mean. Thus the spread is 50 – (-51) or 101 and the biggest deviation is -51. Thus they recorded 101 over -51. For another example, consider Ekaterinoslav with the top number 181 and the lower number 108. Here we subtract 108 from 181 to get 73. That must be the negative deviation to get a spread of 181. That corresponds with scale for Ekaterinoslav in Diagram No. 1.

The notation on this map for Oriol appears to be 58 over 30. But according to Diagram No. 1 in this chapter it should be about 53 over -28. I gave preference to Map 14 and put 58 over 30 on the map.

The names on this map and the names on Diagram No. 1 are not all the same for a given province. By reviewing List A in the Preliminaries, you can match up the names.

Map 15: Localities with an Excess or Deficiency of Grain Crops.

They accidentally colored Lake Ladoga (just northeast of St. Petersburg) on this map in IR.

Diagrams 1a and 1b: Minimal and Maximal Deviations of the Rye Crop from the Average in Per Cents from 1881 to 1891 inclusive, per Government.

Astrakhan is missing from this diagram in IR.

The diagrams and maps in IR were based on numbers derived from surveys and hence are approximations. In redoing the diagrams, I read those approximations on the diagrams as best I could but this produced another approximation and then I located marks on my diagrams by an approximate process! So we should not try to interpret the diagrams precisely.

Diagram 2: Chronology of Russian Crops

This is labeled as Chapter VI, Production of Cereals. But in the narrative and other diagrams and maps of my copy of IR, Chapter VI is called Breadstuffs.

In Diagrams 2–4, I converted the scales from tchertverts per dessiatine (or tchertverts) to bushels per acre (or bushels).

Diagram 5: Harvest with Deduction of Seed.

The bar for wheat in 1891 is difficult to interpret. Perhaps they mean that the harvest less the seed is negative but there was enough old crop to export.

55

AREA UNDER RYE IN PERCENTAGE OF THE
WHOLE CULTIVATED SURFACE.

Chapter VI. Breadstuffs, Map No.1.

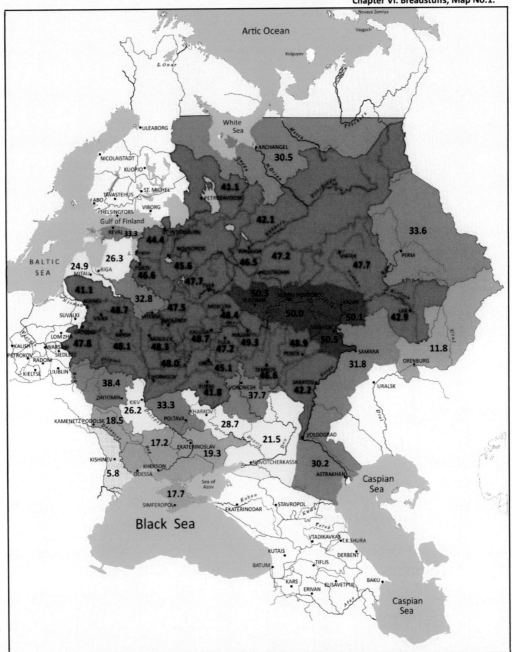

Based on work by D. Semenov and cartographical works by A. Jlyne S.P.B.

Average yearly proportion of land under rye in percentage of the cultivated area.

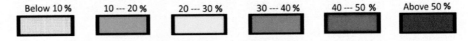

| Below 10 % | 10 --- 20 % | 20 --- 30 % | 30 --- 40 % | 40 --- 50 % | Above 50 % |

The figures on the map show the percentage with greater precision.

AREA UNDER WHEAT IN PERCENTAGE OF THE WHOLE CULTIVATED SURFACE.

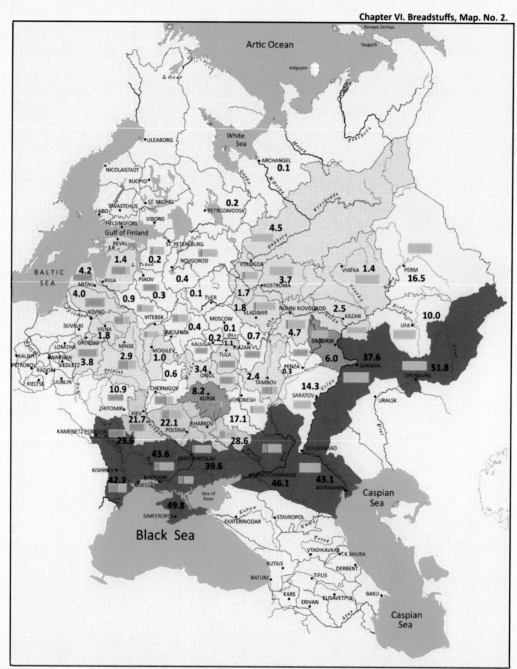

Based on work by D. Semenov and cartographical works by A. Jlyne S.P.B.

Average yearly proportion of land under wheat in percentage of the cultivated area.

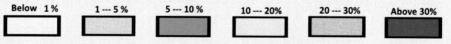

| Below 1 % | 1 --- 5 % | 5 --- 10 % | 10 --- 20% | 20 --- 30% | Above 30% |

The figures on the map show the percentage with greater precision.

The colored (tan and green) rectangles show the proportion of winter wheat (tan) to spring wheat (green).

AREA UNDER OATS IN PERCENTAGE OF THE
WHOLE CULTIVATED SURFACE.

Chapter VI. Breadstuffs, Map No. 3.

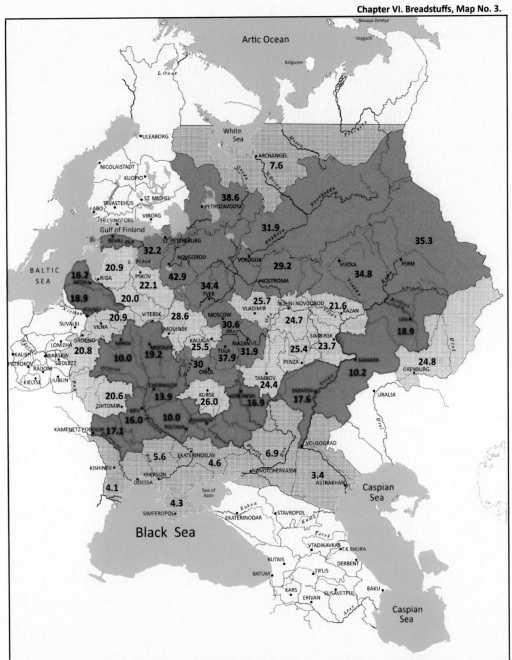

Based on work by A. Fortunatov and cartographical works by A. Jlyne S.P.B.

Average yearly proportion of land under oats in percentage of the cultivated area.

Below 10%	10 --- 20%	20 --- 30%	Above 30%

The figures on the map show the percentage with greater precision.

AREA UNDER BARLEY IN PERCENTAGE OF THE WHOLE CULTIVATED SURFACE.

Chapter VI. Breadstuffs, Map No. 4.

Based on work by D. Semenov and cartographical works by A. Jlyne S.P.B.

Average yearly proportion of land under barley in percentage of the cultivated area.

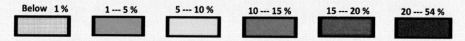

| Below 1% | 1 --- 5 % | 5 --- 10 % | 10 --- 15 % | 15 --- 20 % | 20 --- 54 % |

AREA UNDER MILLET IN PRCENTAGE OF THE
WHOLE CULTIVATED SURFACE.

Chapter VI. Breadstuffs, Map No. 5.

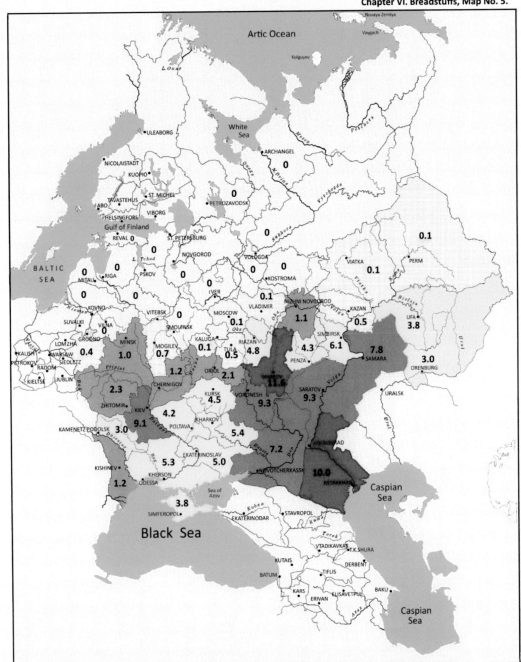

Based on work by D. Semenov and cartographical works by A. Jlyne S.P.B.

Average yearly proportion of land under millet in percentage of the
cultivated area.

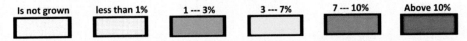

| Is not grown | less than 1% | 1 --- 3% | 3 --- 7% | 7 --- 10% | Above 10% |

AREA UNDER BUCKWHEAT IN PERCENTAGE OF
THE WHOLE CULTIVATED SURFACE.

Chapter VI. Breadstuffs, Map No. 6.

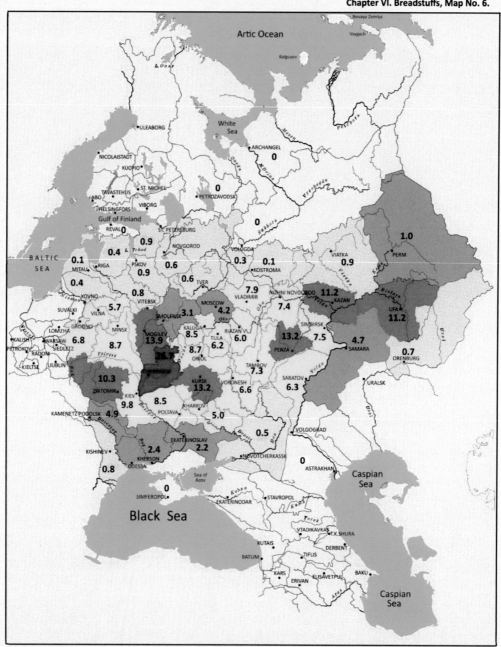

Based on the work by D. Semenov and cartographical works by A. Jlyne S.P.B.

Average yearly proportion of land under buckwheat in percentage of the
cultivated area.

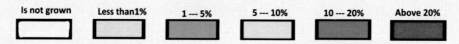

Is not grown	Less than1%	1 --- 5%	5 --- 10%	10 --- 20%	Above 20%

AREA UNDER INDIAN CORN AND SPELT IN
PERCENTAGE OF THE WHOLE CULTIVATED SURFACE.

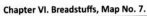
Chapter VI. Breadstuffs, Map No. 7.

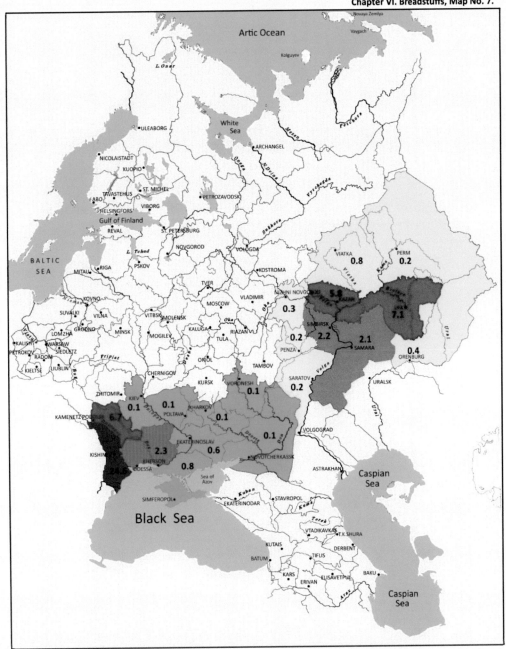

Based on the work of D. Semenov and cartographical work by A. Jlyne S.P.B.

Average yearly proportion of land under Indian Corn or Spelt in
percentage of the cultivated area.

Indian Corn				Spelt		
Below 1%	1 --- 5 %	5 --- 20%	Above 20%	Below 1%	1 --- 5%	Above 5%

AREA UNDER POTATOES IN PERCENTAGE OF
THE WHOLE CULTIVATED SURFACE.

Chapter VI. Breadstuffs, Map No. 8.

Based on the work by D. Semenov and cartographical works by A. Jlyne S.P.B.

Average yearly proportion of land under potatoes in percentage of the cultivated area.

Below 1 %	1 --- 2%	2 --- 4%	4 --- 6%	6 --- 10%	Above 10%

PREVAILING CROPS.

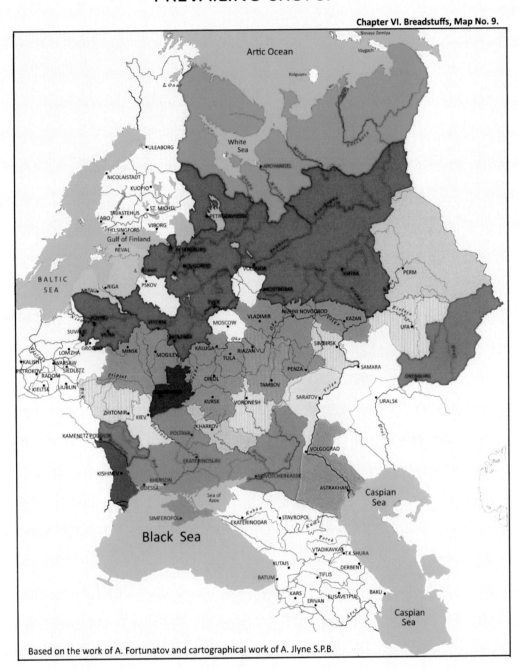

Division of cultivated area according to the three prevailing crops (1886).

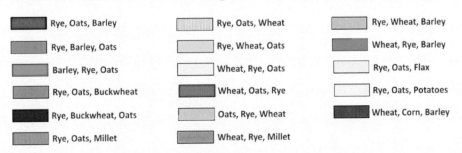

AVERAGE YIELD OF RYE.

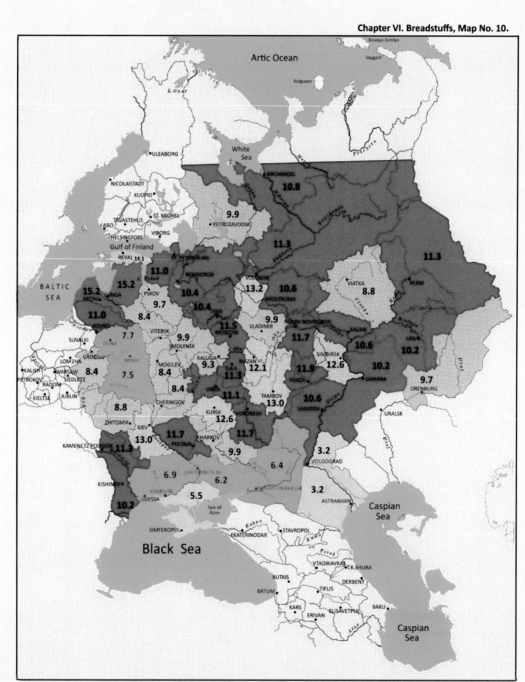

Based on work by D. Semenov and cartographical works by A. Jlyne S.P.B.

Bushels per acre.

| Below 6.07 | 6.07 --- 7.73 | 7.73 --- 9.94 | 9.94 --- 12.15 | 12.15 --- 14.91 | Above 14.91 |

AVERAGE YIELD OF SPRING WHEAT

Chapter VI. Breadstuffs, Map No. 11.

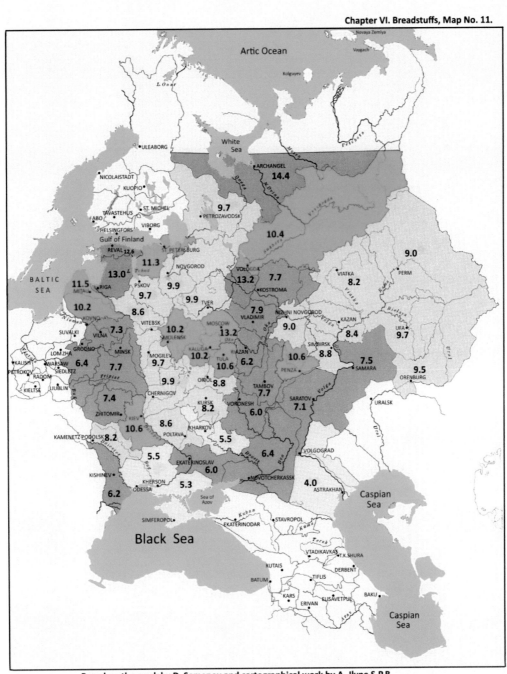

Based on the work by D. Semenov and cartographical work by A. Jlyne S.P.B.

Bushels per acre.

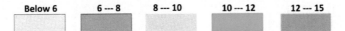

| Below 6 | 6 --- 8 | 8 --- 10 | 10 --- 12 | 12 --- 15 |

AVERAGE YIELD OF OATS.

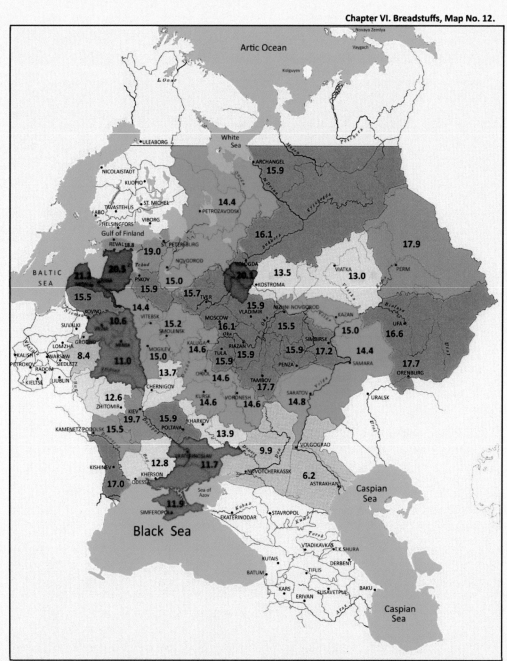

Based on the work by D. Semenov and cartographical works by A. Jlyne St. Pbg.

Bushels per acre.

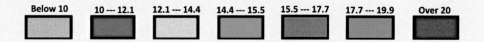

Below 10	10 --- 12.1	12.1 --- 14.4	14.4 --- 15.5	15.5 --- 17.7	17.7 --- 19.9	Over 20

AVERAGE YIELD OF POTATOES.

Based on the work by D. Semenov and cartographical work by A. Jlyne S.P.B.

Bushels per acre

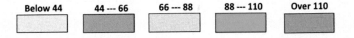

| Below 44 | 44 --- 66 | 66 --- 88 | 88 --- 110 | Over 110 |

YEARLY DEVIATION IN PERCENTAGE OF THE MEAN YIELD OF RYE FOR A PERIOD OF 11 YEARS [1881 - 1891].

Chapter VI. Breadstuffs, Map. No. 14.

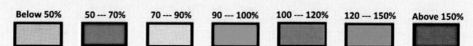

Based on the work by D. Semenov and cartographical works by A. Jlyne St. Pbg.

The top number is the spread between the highest and lowest deviation from the mean. The bottom number is the largest deviation from the mean.

| Below 50% | 50 --- 70% | 70 --- 90% | 90 --- 100% | 100 --- 120% | 120 --- 150% | Above 150% |

LOCALITIES WITH AN EXCESS OR DEFICIENCY
OF GRAIN CROPS.

Chapter VI. Breadstuffs, Map No. 15.

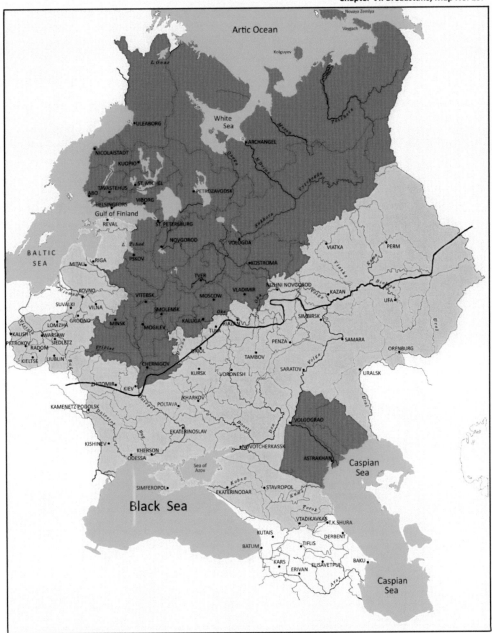

Based on the work by D. Semenov and cartographical works by A. Jlyne St. Pbg.

Localities with an average
excess of grain crops

Localities where imported
grain is consumed

MINIMAL AND MAXIMAL DEVIATIONS OF THE RYE

crop from the average in per cents from 1881 to 1891 inclusive,
per government.

Chapter VI. Breadstuffs, Diagram No. 1a.

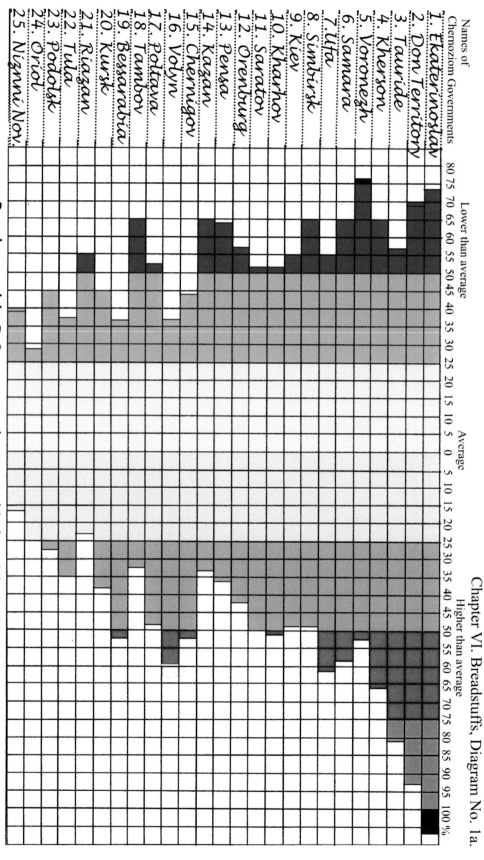

Names of
Chernozìom Governments

1. Ekaterinoslav
2. Don Territory
3. Tauride
4. Kherson
5. Voronezh
6. Samara
7. Ufa
8. Simbírsk
9. Kiev
10. Kharkov
11. Saratov
12. Orenburg
13. Pensa
14. Kazan
15. Chernigov
16. Volyn
17. Poltava
18. Tambov
19. Besarabia
20. Kursk
21. Riazan
22. Tula
23. Podolsk
24. Oríol
25. Nìzhnì Nov.

Lower than average
80 75 70 65 60 55 50 45 40 35 30 25 20 15 10 5

Average
0 5 10 15 20 25 30 35 40 45 50 55 60 65 70 75 80 85 90 95 100 %

Higher than average

Based on work by D. Semenov and cartographical work by A. Jlyne S.P.B.

71

MINMAL AND MAXIMAL DEVIATIONS OF THE RYE
crop from the average in per cents from 1881 to 1891 inclusive,
per government.

Chapter VI. Breadstuffs, Diagram No. 1b.

Names of Non-Chernoziom Governments		
26. Minsk		
27. Mogilev		
28. Yaroslav		
29. Courland		
30. Tver		
31. Kovno		
32. Vitebsk		
33. Pskov		
34. Grodno		
35. Vladimir		
36. Perm		
37. Smolensk		
38. St. Petersburg		
39. Moscow		
40. Kaluga		
41. Viatka		
42. Vologda		
43. Livland		
44. Kostroma		
45. Novgorod		
46. Olonetsk		
47. Vilna		
48. Estland		
49. Archangel		

Lower than average Average Higher than average

80 75 70 65 60 55 50 45 40 35 30 25 20 15 10 5 0 5 10 15 20 25 30 35 40 45 50 55 60 65 70 75 80 85 90 95 100 %

Based on work by D. Semenov and cartographical work by A. Jlyne S.P.B.

CHRONOLOGY OF RUSSIAN CROPS

(1840 – 1889)

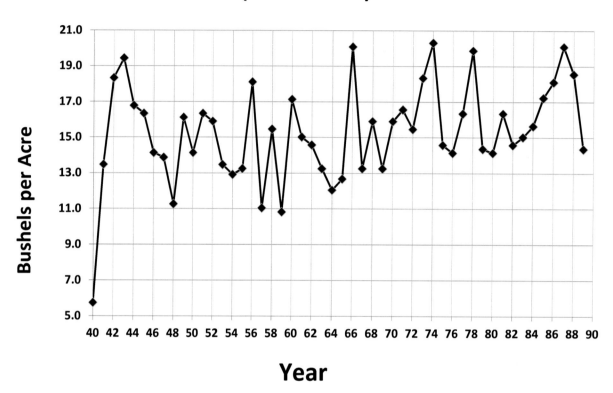

Crops of cereals as per records of private farms of European Russia according to materials gathered by A. Fortunatov and L. I. Grass. Composed by A. Fortunatov and A. Jlin ST PBG

Chapter VI. Breadstuffs, Diagram No. 2.

TOTAL QUANTITY OF DIFFERENT CEREALS

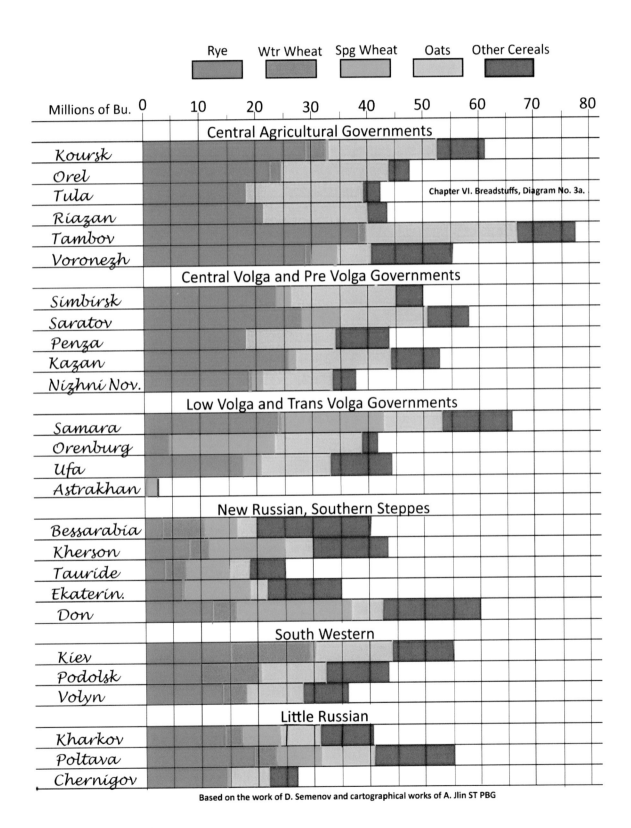

Based on the work of D. Semenov and cartographical works of A. Jlin ST PBG

TOTAL QUANTITY OF DIFFERENT CEREALS

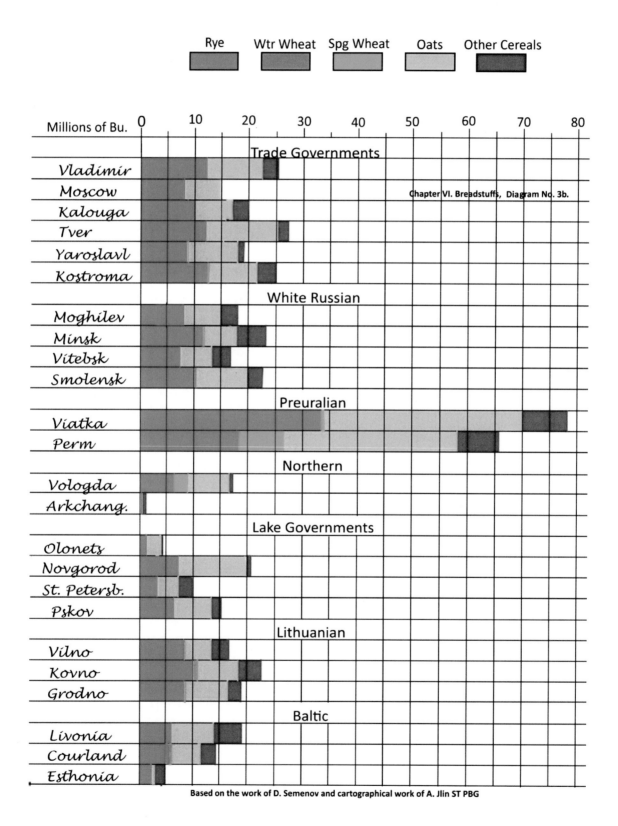

Based on the work of D. Semenov and cartographical work of A. Jlin ST PBG

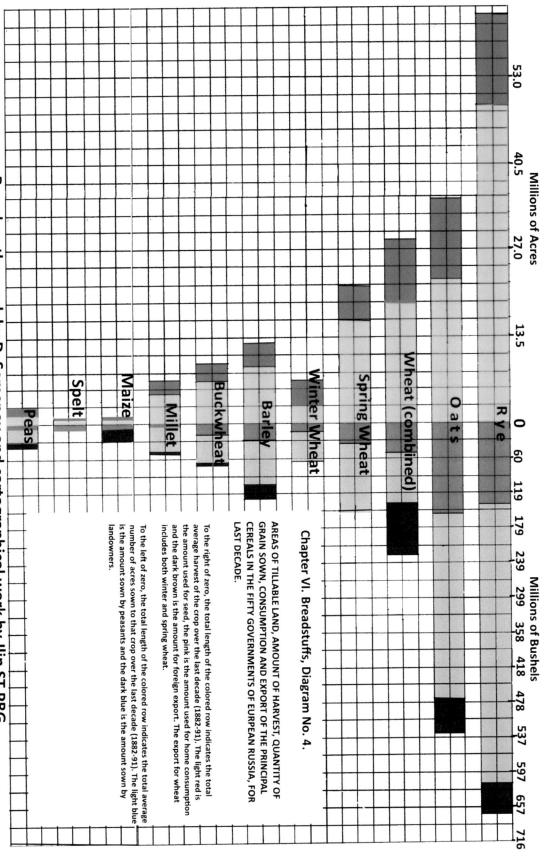

Chapter VI. Breadstuffs, Diagram No. 4.

AREAS OF TILLABLE LAND, AMOUNT OF HARVEST, QUANTITY OF GRAIN SOWN, CONSUMPTION AND EXPORT OF THE PRINCIPAL CEREALS IN THE FIFTY GOVERNMENTS OF EURPEAN RUSSIA, FOR LAST DECADE.

To the right of zero, the total length of the colored row indicates the total average harvest of the crop over the last decade (1882-91). The light red is the amount used for seed, the pink is the amount used for home consumption and the dark brown is the amount for foreign export. The export for wheat includes both winter and spring wheat.

To the left of zero, the total length of the colored row indicates the total average number of acres sown to that crop over the last decade (1882-91). The light blue is the amount sown by peasants and the dark blue is the amount sown by landowners.

Millions of Acres

53.0   40.5   27.0   13.5

Millions of Bushels

0   60   119   179   239   299   358   418   478   537   597   657   716

Rye

Oats

Wheat (combined)

Spring Wheat

Winter Wheat

Barley

Buckwheat

Millet

Maize

Spelt

Peas

Based on the work by D. Semenov and cartographical work by Jlin ST PBG.

HARVEST WITH DEDUCTION OF SEED

and export of the three principal crops for the last nine years.

The length of the rows indicates the amount of harvest with deduction of seed and the dark part indicates the amount of export.

Chapter VI. Breadstuffs, Diagram No. 5.

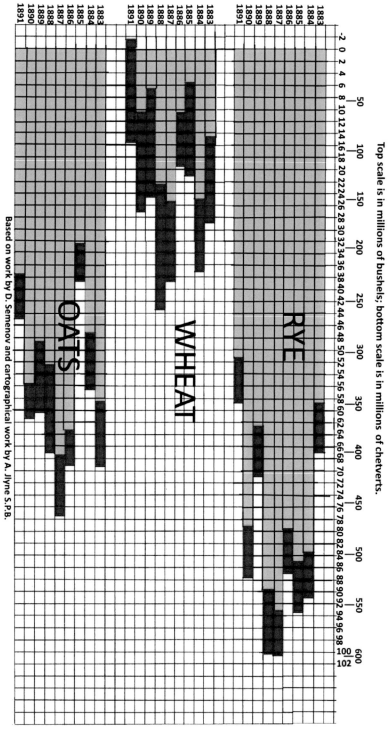

Top scale is in millions of bushels; bottom scale is in millions of chetverts.

Based on work by D. Semenov and cartographical work by A. Jlyne S.P.B.

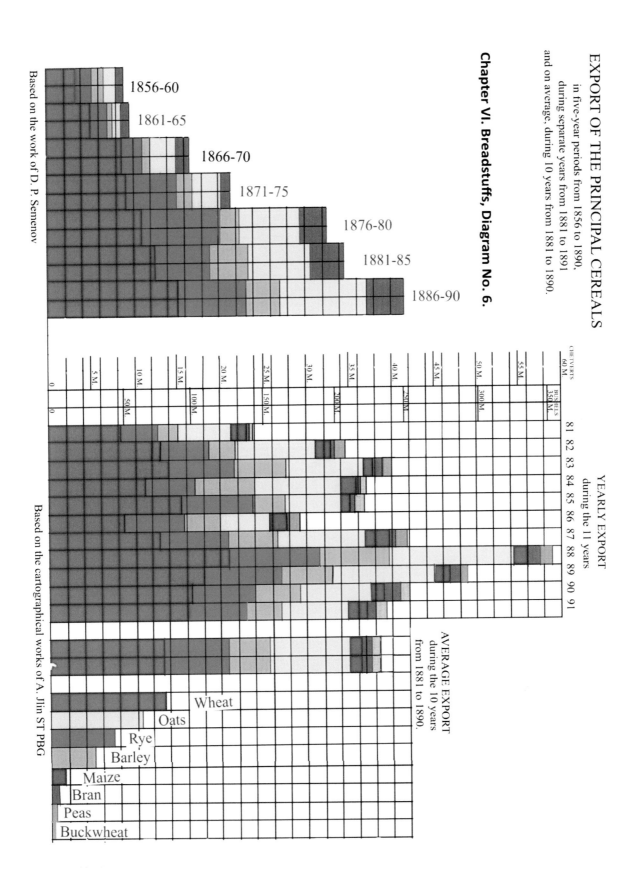

EXPORT OF THE PRINCIPAL CEREALS

in five-year periods from 1856 to 1890,
during separate years from 1881 to 1891
and on average, during 10 years from 1881 to 1890.

Chapter VI. Breadstuffs, Diagram No. 6.

Based on the work of D. P. Semenov

1856-60

1861-65

1866-70

1871-75

1876-80

1881-85

1886-90

CHETVERTS
60 M.
55 M.
50 M.
45 M.
40 M.
35 M.
30 M.
25 M.
20 M.
15 M.
10 M.
5 M.
0

BUSHELS
350 M.
300 M.
250 M.
200 M.
150 M.
100 M.
50 M.
0

YEARLY EXPORT
during the 11 years

81 82 83 84 85 86 87 88 89 90 91

AVERAGE EXPORT
during the 10 years
from 1881 to 1890.

Based on the cartographical works of A. Ilin ST PBG

Wheat

Oats

Rye

Barley

Maize

Bran

Peas

Buckwheat

Chapter VII. Grain Trade.

Highlights:

After grain leaves the farmer, it passes through a number of middlemen such as shippers and processors until it reaches the consumer. At each step commissions and tariffs are charged. This industry is called the grain trade in IR.

The amount of grain exported depends on the crops at home as well as the crops in other exporting countries. It also depends on the demand in the importing countries. So fluctuation in the annual export of grain is common. See for example, the yearly export part of Diagram 6 in Chapter VI.

The left part of the same diagram shows the smoothing effect if five year averages are used and also shows the steady increase of exports of grain from 1856 to 1890.

"The steady development of the export of grain was retarded by a series of bad crops beginning with 1880; thereafter, it has steadily and rapidly increased. In the middle of the seventies, with the development of the southern railroads, the yearly average of export amounted to 200 million pouds; in the five years from 1882 to 1886 it was more than 300 million pouds; in the years from 1885 to 1890 it reached 400 millions, the year 1888 being especially remarkable by its export of more than 540 million poud"(112).

Crops were poor in 1889 but the stores left over from 1888 allowed for a large amount of export. But the crops were still poor in 1890 and very poor in 1891 and, consequently, exports dropped off in those years.

The monetary value of grain exports depends on prices at home and abroad as well as on currency exchange rates. Diagrams1a, 1b, 2, 3 and 4 display some of those relationships. Note the sharp pickup in prices in late 1891 as the extent of the poor crop became known. Note also that prices are higher in seaports such as St. Petersburg, Odessa and Rostov-on-Don than at interior points such as Elects and Saratov. And prices are highest near a point of consumption such as London (Diagram 1a) or Berlin (Diagram 2).

The principal exporting points in Russia can be collected into five groups: The White Sea port, Baltic ports, overland ports and the Black Sea and Azov Sea ports. The only port on the White Sea is at Archangel and it exports only a small amount of oats. The Baltic ports include St. Petersburg, Reval, Riga and Libau. The first of these has been important for a long time because of the waterways to which it is connected. Reval and Libau became important after they got connected to railroads.

Overland exporting points also gained importance with the coming of rail service. The primary ones are at the towns of Virballen, Graevo and Mlava. The Black Sea and Azov ports include Odessa, Nikolaev, Sebastopol, Novorossisk, Rostov-on-Don, Taganrog, Marioupol and Berdiansk. Batum and Poti were minor grain exporting ports on the eastern shores of the Black Sea.

The abridged table for exports in the Remarks section gives the amount of cereals exported from each of these ports in 1889. A more extensive table for all cereals and the years 1886–92 appears in IR on pages 122–123.

The principal importers of grain from Russia are Great Britain, France, Germany, Holland, Belgium and Italy. An abridged table derived from the one on page 132 of IR is displayed in the Remarks section and shows amounts imported by these countries.

Remarks:

Note: Recall that a poud is equivalent to 32.243 English pounds. Libau (Liepata) is a town on the Baltic Sea southwest of Riga. It is in the country of Latvia now as is Riga. Poti and Batoum (Batum) are in Georgia on the east coast of the Black Sea. Novorossisk is also on the east coast of the Black Sea about three-fourths of the way from Sochi to Kerch. I was not able to pinpoint the location of Virballen,

Graevo and Mlava. In 1890 presumably they were on the frontier between Russia and Eastern Europe.

I chose the year 1889 for the following tables as it seemed to be more typical than other years in the late 1880s or early 1890s.

Export of all cereals from ports in 1889 in millions of pouds (122–123).

Port	Amount	Percent of Total
St. Petersburg and Cronstadt	32.8	8.5
Reval	12.1	3.1
Riga	15.7	4.1
Libau	38.9	10.1
Virballen, Graevo, Mlava	25.0	6.5
Odessa	105.7	27.4
Nikolaev	33.0	8.5
Sebastopol	26.0	6.7
Berdiansk	13.5	3.5
Marioupol	8.4	2.2
Taganrog	15.4	4.0
Rostov-on-Don	39.7	10.3
Novorossisk	15.4	4.0
Poti	4.0	1.0
Batoum	0.7	0.2
Total	386.3	100*

*The numbers in the last column do not total 100 due to rounding off.

These numbers show the relative importance of the Black Sea (including the Azov Sea) ports and nearby farmers in the production of cereals for export.

Principal destinations of Russian grain exports in 1889 in millions of pouds (132).

Country	Wheat	Rye	Oats	Barley
Great Britain	66.1	---	43.3	24.4
France	23.1	0.5	5.8	3.6
Germany	18.3	55.6	14.5	18.3
Holland	15.9	23.4	7.0	4.4
Belgium	6.6	1.7	7.6	5.6
Italy	38.6	---	---	5.6

Diagrams 1a, 1b, 2, 3 and 4 show the prices of wheat, rye, barley and oats in kopecks per poud at various grade trading centers in Russia and Western Europe. I did not change kopecks to US dollars or pouds to bushels because these diagrams are useful in the given units for observing trends and relationships and little would be gained by converting to other units.

For example, prices of all grains shot up in the summer and fall of 1891 verifying that the harvest was poor that year. In Diagram 1b, we can see that the price for wheat in Saratov hovered around 75 paper kopecks per poud in 1889 and 1890 but increased to nearly double that amount by the end of 1891. The price of rye in Saratov in 1889 and 1890 was in the high 50s according to Diagram 2. But it increased to about 130 by late 1891, an increase of almost 200%.

By studying the diagrams in this chapter and Diagrams 5 and 6 in Chapter VI, some interesting deductions can be made about crop and market conditions in the years 1889–92.

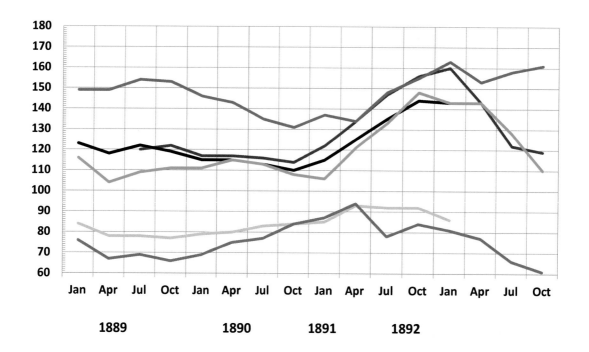

Variation in the price of wheat per poud.

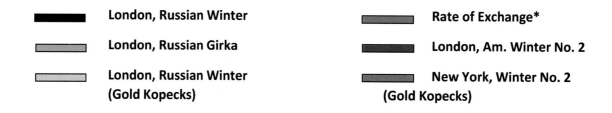

	London, Russian Winter		Rate of Exchange*
London, Russian Girka		London, Am. Winter No. 2
London, Russian Winter (Gold Kopecks)		New York, Winter No. 2 (Gold Kopecks)

Variations in the price of wheat in the markets shown for the years 1889, 1890, 1891 and 1892 in kopecks (paper/gold) per poud. Chart is based on Diagram No. 1 in Chapter VII of IR produced by P. A. Shostak and A. Jlyne ST PBG.

*Rate of exchange in paper kopecks per gold rouble

Chapter VII. Grain Trade, Diagram 1a.

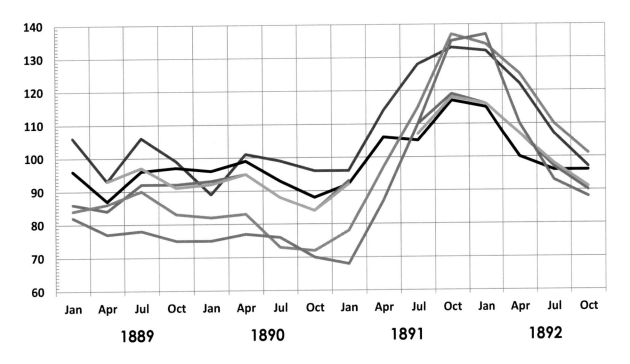

Variation in the price of wheat per poud.

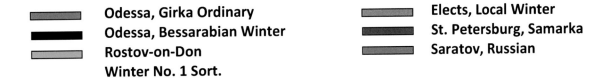

Odessa, Girka Ordinary
Odessa, Bessarabian Winter
Rostov-on-Don
Winter No. 1 Sort.

Elects, Local Winter
St. Petersburg, Samarka
Saratov, Russian

Variations in the price of wheat in the markets shown for the years 1889, 1890, 1891 and 1892 in paper kopecks per poud. Chart is based on Diagram No. 1 in Chapter VII of IR produced by P. A. Shostak and A. Jlyne ST PBG.

Chapter VII. Grain Trade, Diagram 1b.

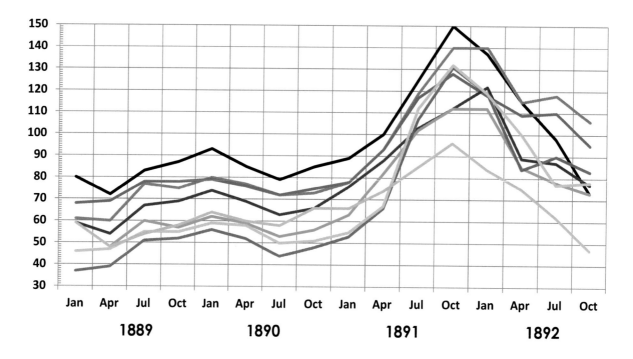

Variation in the price of rye per poud.

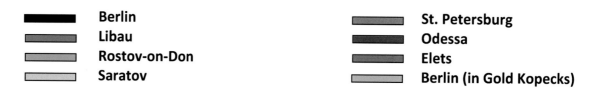

	Berlin		St. Petersburg
	Libau		Odessa
	Rostov-on-Don		Elets
	Saratov		Berlin (in Gold Kopecks)

Variations in the price of rye in the markets shown for the years 1889, 1890, 1891 and 1892 in kopecks (paper/gold) per poud. Chart is based on Diagram No. 2 in Chapter VII of IR produced by P. A. Shostak and A. Jlyne PBG.

Chapter VII. Grain Trade, Diagram 2.

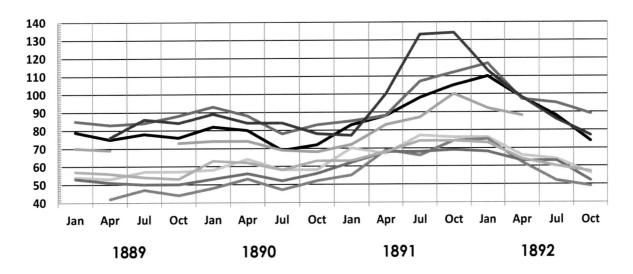

Variation in the price of barley per poud.

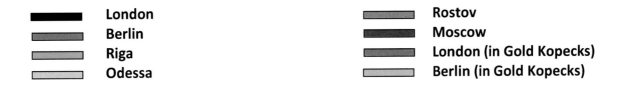

Variations in the price of barley in the markets shown for the years 1889, 1890, 1891 and 1892 in kopecks (paper/gold) per poud. Chart is based on Diagram No. 3 in Chapter VII of IR produced by P. A. Shostak and A. Jlyne S.P.B.

Chapter VII. Grain Trade, Diagram 3.

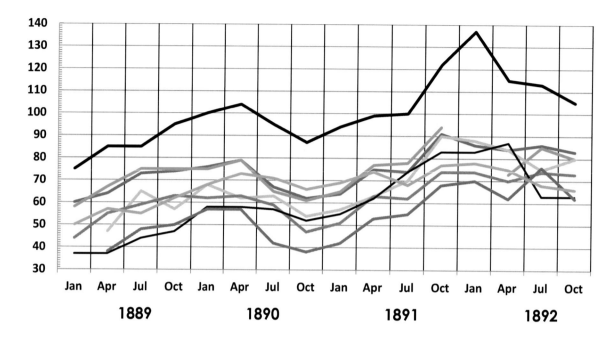

Variation in the price of oats per poud.

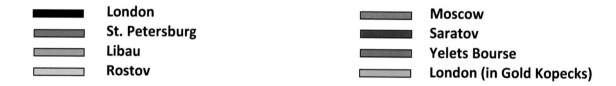

London		Moscow	
St. Petersburg		Saratov	
Libau		Yelets Bourse	
Rostov		London (in Gold Kopecks)	

Variations in the price of oats in the markets shown for the years 1889, 1890, 1891 and 1892 in kopecks (paper/gold) per poud. Chart is based on Diagram No. 2 in Chapter VII of IR produced by P. A. Shostak and A. Jlyne S.P.B.

Chapter VII. Grain Trade, Diagram 4.

Chapter VIII. Other Field Produce.

Highlights:

Flax:

For a long time flax has been grown and used for the making of cloth and for the oil in its seed. It became an item of trade in the sixteenth century. By 1870, 11.5 million pouds of flax and tow (partially processed flax fiber) were exported.

Map 1 in this chapter shows the primary flax growing regions of European Russia.

Flax grown in non-chernoziom areas is long-stemmed and valuable for fiber. The flax grown in chernoziom regions is shorter and produces more grain.

The value of flax for fiber has gradually decreased from 1862 to 1890 because more products are being made with cotton.

Germany and Great Britain are the primary importers of flax fiber and tow. Flax seed is sent to Great Britain, Germany, Holland, Belgium, Denmark, France and Sweden.

Hemp:

Russia produces about 40% of the hemp produced in Europe.

Map 2 in this chapter gives the principal areas of hemp production in Russia.

Two-thirds of Russian hemp goes to Germany and more than half of the rest to Great Britain. Hemp, like flax, is losing its importance due competition from cotton and Manila hemp.

Cotton:

"In Russia the cotton plant is grown in Turkestan and beyond the Caucasus" (143). After 1860 the production of cotton decreased rapidly in Russia due to depressed prices and competition from abroad.

Sunflower:

At first sunflowers were grown for the seed for food mainly in the government of Saratov. However in the 1830s the peasant Bokarev discovered that the seed contained a large amount of oil and that this oil had many uses.

"When the plants are an arshine high, the side branches are cut off to encourage the growth of the heads and the filling of the seed. The sunflower when ripe is cut down with a hook, and after drying on the field in order to facilitate the separation of the seeds from the heads, is gathered and hauled to the thrashing-floors where it is thrashed; that which is destined for the production of oil is thrashed with flails, that which is to be eaten as a nut, with sticks, the heads being placed in several rows one upon another to avoid damage to the hulls of the seed" (150).

For 1886 and 1887 the main sunflower-growing areas are given in this table (151):

Government	Dessiatines/Per Year
Voronesh	100,963
Saratov	83,860
Tambov	24,557
Kursk	15,143
Samara	9,510
Don Territory	5,452
Kharkov	5,225
Poltava	4,767

The oil and seed are used locally but some of the residue is exported for fodder for cattle and fowl. Prices for both the seed and oil have fallen a great deal in the last several years.

Rape Seed, Surepka and Repak:

These crops are grown mostly by landowners rather than by peasants and are of little significance economically.

Mustard:

The center of mustard production is Sarepta, the German colony in the Tsaritsyn district of the Saratov government. From there the cultivation of mustard has spread to the governments of Astrakhan, Don and some other places in southern Russia.

"In the middle of the forties there were built three new oil mills in Sarepta and Dubovka by various persons from among the Colonists. In 1850 came the first steam mill in consequence of which the production considerably increased. In 1864, a second steam mill was brought into operation also in Sarepta, in 1870, two more steam mills in Dubovka, in 1884, others arose in Dubovka, Tsaritsyn and Sarepta, and finally, in 1888, a new mill was built in Tsaritsyn" (155).

Garden Cress (Ryzhik):

This plant is grown for its seed from which oil is extracted and used in food. There is a good demand for it on foreign markets. Only a little is grown, however, and mainly in the governments of Poltava, Chernigov, Kiev, Kherson, Ekaterinoslav and Kursk.

Poppy:

This plant is also grown for the oil in its seed. It is grown in limited quantities all over Russia.

Tobacco:

Plantings and harvests of tobacco vary a great deal from year to year and from region to region. In 1884 only 2.3 million pouds were brought in. But in 1887, 3.4 million pouds were harvested.

Production of tobacco occurs over most of Russia but about 70% of the total crop is grown in the governments of Chernigov, Poltava, Tauride and Kubansk. Bessarabia is also important in tobacco growing.

"Lastly there are localities of the Samara government where tobacco has been raised from ancient times, and where the crop is now concentrated in the German colonies" (159–160).

Although Russia grows enough tobacco to supply local needs and to support some exporting, the quality of its tobacco is low. Thus some higher quality tobacco is imported to mix with the Russian tobacco. Cigars are also imported.

"Tobacco of the highest grades are mostly cultivated in the south of European Russia, namely in the governments of Bessarabia and Tauride, and in the Caucasus" (160).

However the number of fertile fields in Bessarabia has diminished to the point that tobacco production has decreased lately.

Beets:

"Beet culture, for obtaining sugar, has existed in Russia from the beginning of the present century. It came from Germany, and from the year 1800 [when] lands were distributed free of cost in the southern regions of Russia to persons who wished to engage in this branch of agriculture" (164).

The beet industry has progressed slowly. But by now it is well developed. In the principal governments where beets are grown, the per cent of sown land devoted to beets in 1883 was as follows (165): Kiev (4.99%), Podolsk (3.62%), Kharkov (1.56%), Kursk (1.01%) and Volinia (1.04%). In the years 1886 to 1892, the governments of Samara, Ekaterinoslav and Bessarabia were relatively small beet producers. However the yields per dessiatine were higher in Bessarabia than anywhere else in Russia.

Beets have to be grown near refineries because transporting them over poorly maintained roads in the fall is expensive. Other expenses and labor involved in raising beets are also high.

The French varieties of beets contain more and better sugar whereas the German varieties produce a larger root.

Hops:

Hops are grown in small quantities all over European Russia. It can be used to make a low quality beer and Russian Braga (a Russian beer). For brewing better beer higher quality hops are imported. This has attracted the attention of the government which has taken steps to improve the quality of Russian hops.

Aniseed and Cumin:

Aniseed is grown commercially in only a few places in Russia. Those places include Voronesh, Koursk, Kharkov, Tauride and Kherson. Part of the crop is rendered into oil and used as medicine or in alcoholic drinks. The rest is exported.

Cumin is cultivated in Yaroslav and neighboring governments.

Mint:

Mint is raised in Yaroslav and Tula and less so in Voronesh, Orel and Kherson. The oil extracted from the leafs and the leafs themselves are used in the preparation of medicines, perfumes, candy and aromatic drinks. It is used, for example, in the Russian kvas.

Chicory:

Chicory is grown for its roots which are used in flavoring of foods. It is grown in the government of Yaroslav and nearby areas as well as in the Baltic region.

Teasel:

A small amount of teasel is grown in Minsk, Bessarabia and Crimea. It is used in the manufacture of cloth.

Remarks:

A dessiatine, as mentioned before, is about 2.7 acres. An arshine is equivalent to 28 inches. A poud is about 32.24 pounds.

Sarepta was a German village settled in 1765–73 by Moravian Brethren who were weavers from Germany. They introduced the industry of cloth-making to the lower Volga area.

Dubovka was a German village. It was a daughter colony of the original Volga German colonies.

Tsaritsyn is an old name for Volgograd which is a new name for Stalingrad.

Raising and harvesting tobacco can be done in many different ways. See, for example, pages 162–164 of IR.

Beet culture is described in detail in pages 168–170 in IR.

In IR, Maps 1 and 2 of this chapter were based on dessiatines per 100 square versts. That is an odd choice of units even for that time and place. (A verst is about 2/3 of a mile.) I recast both maps in terms of the more familiar units of acres per 10,000 acres.

CULTIVATION OF FLAX.

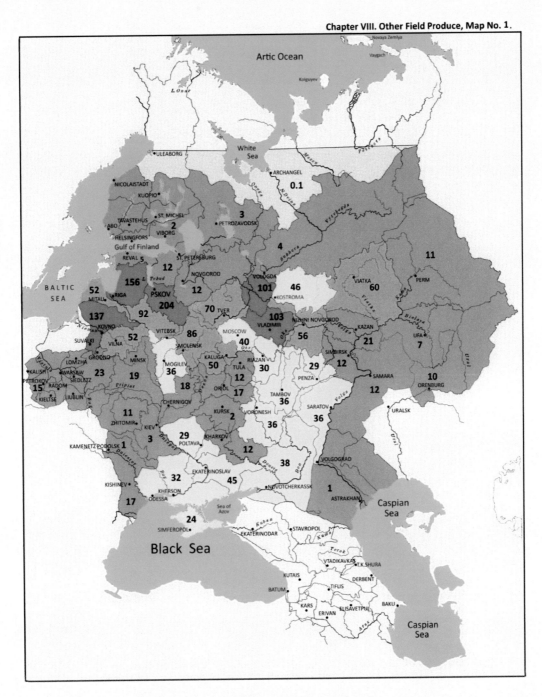

Total area occupied by flax in 1886 in each government
in acres per 10,000 acres.

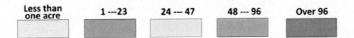

| Less than one acre | 1 --- 23 | 24 --- 47 | 48 --- 96 | Over 96 |

CULTIVATION OF HEMP.

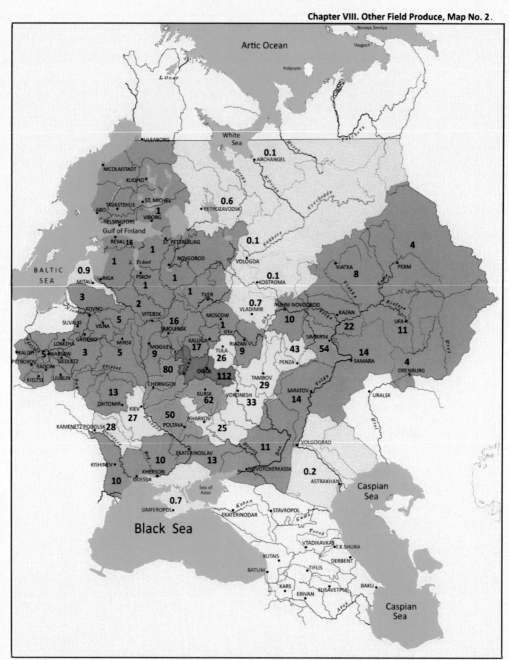

Based on the work by A. A. Blau and cartographical works by A. Jlyne St. Pbg.

Total area occupied by hemp in 1886 in each government in acres per 10,000 acres.

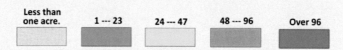

Less than one acre.	1 --- 23	24 --- 47	48 --- 96	Over 96

Chapter IX. Gardens and Viticulture.

Highlights:

Gardening:

Gardening for home use has been important in Russia for a long time. With the coming of the railroad and some processing capability, raising garden and orchard products for sale has slowly gained strength. The principal reason for the slow development is the lack of technical knowledge in the rural population.

The most popular vegetables are cabbage, cucumbers, onions and melons. Sour cabbage and salted cucumbers are common food items among the peasantry. Pumpkins, red peppers, garlic, cumin, fenel, tomatoes, peas, beans, maize, sunflowers, asparagus and chicory are also grown.

Melon fields are called bashtani or bakchi. The produce from those fields is sold locally and in nearby towns. This industry is most developed in the governments of Saratov, Samara, Astrakhan and the Don territory.

In the southern steppes, gardening is most advanced around Odessa, Nicolaev, in some districts of Bessarabia, along the Dnieper River and by Rostov-on-Don. Kharkov and Voronezh also deserve mention.

"Of the eastern region, gardening is principally developed in the governments of Saratov and Simbirsk. In the vicinity of Saratov, in the Alexandrovsk volost, tomatoes are grown in great quantities, and in the village of Bykovka, cabbage and early potatoes; the former is also much cultivated on the borders of rivers in the districts of Volsk, Serdobsk and on other streams of the Saratov government, where the German colonists grow also many turnips" (184).

Orchards:

"Fruit trees and shrubs grow over all Russia, and sometimes even in the wild state; in the northern part of the country berry bushes, apples and cherries predominate, and towards the south, pears, plums, apricots, grapes, nuts, and peaches. In Asiatic Russia the same is true, except that the limits of the different fruit crops lie more to the south"(189).

Some areas and associated fruits are:

Viborg (in Finland), Vologda, Olonets, Mogilev and Viatka: apples.

Perm, Ufa and Orenburg: cherries.

St. Petersburg, Novgorod: berries (strawberries, currants, gooseberries, blackberries and raspberries).

Koursk: pears.

Poltava: plums and cherries.

Voronezh: apples and cherries.

Bessarabia and Podolsk: prunes, plums and grapes.

Crimea: apples, pears, plums, walnuts, cherries, medlars, quinces, apricots, peaches, almonds, chestnuts, figs and pistachios.

"In the east of Russia, fruit culture has greatly developed on the border of the Volga, especially on the high right bank, and along the rivers which fall into it; also in the governments of Saratov, Simbirsk and Kazan" (190).

The most advanced orchards are in the south-western regions of Russia (Kiev, Podolsk, Bessarabia and western Kherson). Fruit culture is important along the Dniester River.

Viticulture:

"Viticulture is the most developed in the Caucasus, Bessarabia and the Crimea and grapes are less grown for wine in Turkestan, the regions of the Don, and still less in the governments of Kherson, Podolsk, Astrakhan, Ekaterinoslav and the regions of the Ural . . ." (195).

"In the government of Elisavetpol, in which the centres for wine fabrication are the German colonies, Elenendorf and Ekaterinenfeld, there are 7,000 dessiatines under grape which produce yearly 650,000 vedros of wine" (196).

"In Bessarabia, where vine is cultivated from ancient times, even in the second and third century before Christ, there are 70,000 dessiatines in vineyard, which produce yearly more than 12,000,000 vedros of wine. This wine is of a considerably lower quality and is sold as cheap as 20 kopecks to one rouble per vedro" (197).

"The vineyards in Crimea, Government of the Tauride, occupy an area of 7,800 dessiatines, which produce yearly more than 1,500,000 vedros of wine. The vineyards , situated on the southern rocky border of the Crimea, where the soil is of clay-slate, produce wine of such good quality that it is celebrated not only over all Russia, but also abroad" (197).

Remarks:

A vedro is equivalent to 3.249 US gallons. Using that fact we can convert the yields implied in the last three paragraphs of viticulture to the following table:

Government	Gallons of Wine per Acre of Vineyards
Elisavetpol	112
Bessarabia	206
Crimea in Tauride	231

The German colonists in southern Russia called melon fields bashtun. Perhaps they picked up this word from the Russian bashtani.

Chapter X. Live Stock.

Highlights:

Agriculture refers to the raising of crops. Animal husbandry is a separate enterprise although it is often closely tied to agriculture.

The peasants in western Russia put more emphasis on animal husbandry than peasants in other regions because they have more population as customers. Moreover, they need more manure for their closely tended agricultural fields.

Dairy and meat production from cattle are most important in the northwestern governments and the Baltic and Finnish provinces.

Dairy and swine are more common in Vistula (Poland) and western governments.

In the southwest and Bessarabia, dairy, swine, wool production and the raising of work horses and cattle are prominent.

In the east and the Caucasus regions, herding is the primary occupation.

Maps No. 1 and No. 2 show the number of large and small livestock per 100 inhabitants and per 100 dessiatines of fertile soil, respectively. **Remark:** The phrase "fertile soil" is not defined by the authors of IR.

In Russia, livestock becomes smaller as you go north. Weights of some slaughtered animals by region are given in the table below (weights are converted to US pounds). In this table the weights are described as ". . . slaughtered, average weight, together with the fat . . ." except for horses for which the live weight is stated. Northern animals appear to weigh only about half as much as the steppe animals.

Animal	Weights in US Lbs.
Steppe Cattle	571
Great Russian Cattle	226
Steppe Merino Sheep	83
Northern Sheep	41
Swine	250
Horses	580

We now turn to highlights for particular species of animals.

Horses:

In European Russia there are about 25 horses per 100 inhabitants whereas in the US the comparable number is 24. Map 3 gives the number of horses as a percentage of the total number of livestock.

"According to the data of 1888, in the 41 governments of European Russia the peasants owned 81.07 per cent of the total number of horses, the large landowners, 15.5 per cent and the town inhabitants, 2.08 per cent. The same data show that there were 40.1 per cent of peasant households possessing a horse, 31.03 per cent owning 2 horses, and 28.6 per cent, three or more horses. The number of peasant households having no horse formed 29 per cent, of which the greater number were in the south-western governments, and in Little Russia, where the beasts of burden are oxen and cows and not horses; the smallest per cent of households without horses was in the north-western governments" (210).

In 1882, horses were put into three categories by size: those less than 52.5 dumes (inches) and these accounted for 58.8 percent, those between 52.5 and 56 dumes which were 28.5 percent of the total and those over 56 dumes which were 12.7 percent (210).

"As to the breeds and designation of Russian horses, the bulk of them are the peasant and steppe horses. There are very few purely local or foreign breeds in Russia" (210).

Horned Cattle:

Map 4 shows the percentage of livestock that are horned cattle.

"In the northern, north-eastern and central Chernoziom and non-Chernoziom governments the cattle of local origin are small, being more suitable for the dairy than for work or fattening"(213).

"Cattle of the southern steppe, south-western, Little Russian and south-eastern governments are of large size, capable of hard labour, and fatten easily; they are known under the name of steppe cattle"(213).

"The crossing of Ukraine with the Kiansk and Sharolezsk breeds has given good results: the mongrels are of good construction, tall and more easily fattened than Ukraine cattle, and the quality of the meat improved" (214).

Sheep:

The most sheep are raised in Tauride, Astrakhan, Ekaterinoslav, Don and Kouban.

Merino sheep are fine-wool sheep and common sheep are course-wool sheep. In European Russia, Merino are 20% of the total. In the Koubansk, Tersk, Uralsk and Stavropol governments the percentage of Merino sheep is higher.

From 1879 to 1882, the number of Merino and common sheep dropped sharply due to falling prices of wool and decreasing sales of mutton. The poor crops of hay and straw in the southern steppes were also factors.

"During the reign of Catherine II, the breeding of Merinos was still more developed , especially as such rich landowners and influential people as Vorontsov, Roumiantsov, Cochoubei, Nesselrode and others imported the breed from Spain and Saxony. For the working up of merino wool many cloth factories were established in different parts of the empire. The breeding of merinos attained its full development during the reign of Alexander I, who distributed lands, in the southern governments, to foreign sheep breeders. In a short time the industry had such a firm foundation that in 1817 a statute was ordained, prohibiting further distribution of Government lands among private herders" (216–217).

Swine:

As shown on map 6, the number of pigs as a percentage of the total number of livestock is largest in the central-western governments. Swine is raised principally for local consumption.

Trade in Livestock, Meat and Wool:

Trade in livestock is carried on in markets and bazaars. The largest markets are in southern Russia. Fattened cattle are slaughtered in towns and others are bought by farmers and dealers.

"Cattle are fattened principally in the south-western and southern steppes, and also in the Don, Kouban and Ural governments" (219).

"In 1890 about 845,000 head of cattle were transported by Russian railways, of which 193,958 heads were taken to the Moscow market, and 119,375 to that of St. Petersburg" (220).

"The average price of fattened steppe oxen has fluctuated during late years, from 85 to 113 roubles per head; of Russian cattle, from 28 to 51 roubles; of calves, from 14 to 17 roubles; of pigs, from 11 to 19 roubles and of sheep, from 6 to 8 roubles. The town of Odessa is the great point of export of live stock. In 1888, 121,000 head of cattle, and 81,000 of sheep were brought to Odessa for sale" (220).

"In all of European Russia from 7,000,000 to 7,500,000 pouds of unwashed and scoured wool are produced; of this quantity 2,500,000 to 3,000,000 pouds are merino wool" (220).

Remark: A poud equals 32.243 US pounds.

The export of horses has increased by a factor of three from 1881 to 1890.

Dairy Farming:

"In the north of Russia, cow milk is exclusively used, and the south makes all sorts of cheese, principally from sheep milk" (221).

"The milk was taken into the cellar in such wares and placed upon shelves or on the floor to cool and cream. These milk cellars were constructed by digging a pit into the earth over which a little cottage, izba, with shelves on the walls, was built. During the winter, when practical, this pit was filled with ice. In summer all sorts of provisions were kept in such milk houses" (223).

"During the last 25 years more has been done in Russia to further the cheese making industry than in any other country" (226).

"Thus after many years of experiment it has been learned that the best regions for making Swiss cheese are the Caucasus, and in parts of Bessarabia and in the Crimea" (227).

Bird Breeding:

Raising poultry is still very much a local enterprise. Poultry consists of chickens, ducks, geese, turkey and guinea hens (in southern Russia).

Average prices for poultry and eggs during the summer are as follows (229):

Fowl	Price
Hens	20 to 25 kopecks apiece
Chickens	5 to 15 kopecks apiece
Ducks	15 to 30 kopecks apiece
Geese	50 to 70 kopecks apiece
Turkeys	60 to 80 kopecks apiece
Eggs	6 to 10 kopecks for ten

In the winter the prices for these commodities are about double the summer prices.

Bee Culture:

Bee culture and honey have been important since at least the year 1000 CE. "In general, apiculture was of great importance to the economy of the country and to all classes of society, from the peasant to the prince. The products of the industry served not only for home consumption, but were objects of export to many countries of Western Europe. With these products also the people paid their taxes and tributes to the Government" (233).

"In the beginning of the last century, during the reign of Peter the Great, different fiscal measures laid a restraint on bee culture, and probably from that time the industry began to decline. In 1775, the tax, laid by Peter the Great on bee products, was annulled" (234).

Bee and honey culture is now practiced mainly by amateurs in Russia and no longer form a basis for trade.

"In the government of Chernigov, for example, buckwheat is the principal food for bees, and if that cereal fails the bees do not thrive. Generally the abundance or scarcity of honey depends on the condition of field crops, and upon the length of time the crops are in blossom. In case of drought, as in the years 1890 and 1891, from the drying up of the grasses and their defloration, the bees are artificially fed from the beginning of summer, and the harvests of honey and wax are then very small" (235).

The Silkworm Industry:

The silkworm industry is a small part of Russian agriculture. However, the few families that practice it, find it lucrative.

"Silkworms are principally grown in the Transcaucasus, Turkestan, and to a considerable extent, in the Transcaspian territory, in the northern Caucasus and in the southern governments of the Empire. In the Transcaucasus silkworms are cultivated by Tartars, Armenians and Georgians; in Turkestan, by the Sartes; in the Transcaspian regions, by the Tekins; in the north Caucasus, by Cossacks and Armenians; and in the southern governments of Russia, by Russians, Bulgarians, Moldavians and Germans" (237).

"The greatest part of raw silk, produced in Russia, is used by Moscow and its environs, where all kinds of tissues are fabricated from it and which are sent over all the Empire" (239).

Remarks:

Horses:

The numbers in the second paragraph under horses are hard to understand. Perhaps they mean 29 percent owned no horse but of the other 71 percent, 40.1 percent owned one horse, 31.03 percent owned two horses and 28.6 percent owned three or more.

Horned Cattle:

In IR, both Maps No. 1 and No. 2 are titled "Total Number of Cattle." But that title is not accurate according to the legend labels. I used the legends for the titles of the maps.

In Map No. 2, the numbers of large and small livestock are given per 100 dessiatines of fertile soil. If you want to restate the numbers in livestock numbers per 100 acres of fertile soil, simply divide the given numbers by 3 (or more precisely, divide by 2.6997).

In the section on Horned Cattle in IR, nothing is said about the red cattle some claim were introduced into Russia by German colonists. Some information about this and "Red Steppe cattle" can be found at the site www.ansi.okstate.edu/breeds/cattle/redsteppe.

Sheep:

Catherine II came to be known as Catherine the Great and was the first to invite western Europeans, especially German, colonists to the Volga River area. She was czarina of Russia from 1762 to 1796.

Alexander I, the grandson of Catherine the Great, invited western Europeans to the Black Sea region in 1804. Again mainly German speaking people answered the call and in great numbers.

Map number 5 gives the number of sheep as a percentage of the total number of livestock. Notice this percentage is highest in Astrakhan and the southern steppe governments.

Swine:

Map number 6 gives the number of swine as a percentage of the total number of livestock. This percentage is highest in the west-central governments.

Trade in Livestock, Meat and Wool:

For perspective on the prices quoted for various livestock, the price for wheat in Odessa in 1889–90 was about 95 kopecks per poud (see Diagram 1b in Chapter VII). If we divide 95 by 32.243 we get the price per pound of wheat. Then, multiplying by 60, we obtain about 177 kopecks for one bushel of wheat. That is the same as 1.77 roubles per bushel.

Dairy Farming:

The "wares" referred to in the quote from page 223 were glazed clay pitchers.

The milk houses referred to in IR seem to be very much like our root or ice cellars in the US.

Bird Breeding:

By comparison, the price for a bushel of wheat at approximately the same time period in Odessa was about 177 kopecks (1.77 roubles) per bushel. See the calculation above.

The Silkworm Industry:

Turkestan and Transcaspian Territories were just east of the Caspian Sea. Transcaucasus is the area encompassing the present countries of Armenia, Azerbaijan and Georgia.

LIVESTOCK PER 100 INHABITANTS

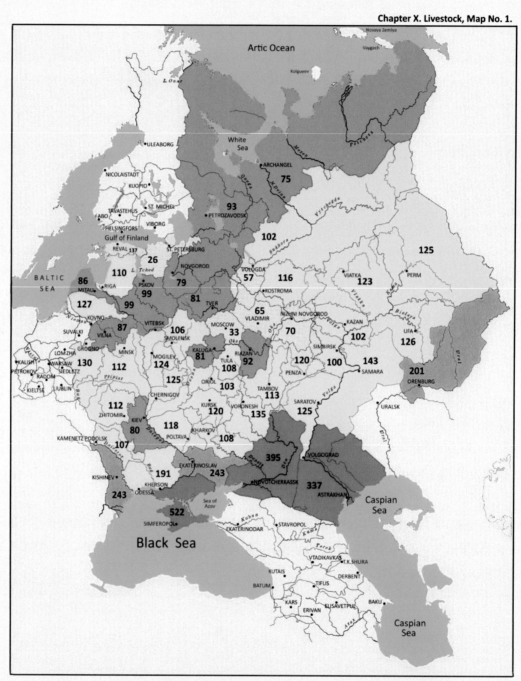

Based on the map from the Statistical Section of the Department of Agriculture and A. Jlyne S.P.B.

Number of large and small livestock per 100 inhabitants.

| Less than 75 | 75 --- 100 | 100 --- 200 | 200 --- 300 | 300 or more |

NUMBER OF LIVESTOCK PER 100 DESSIATINES OF FERTILE SOIL.

Chapter X. Livestock, Map No. 2.

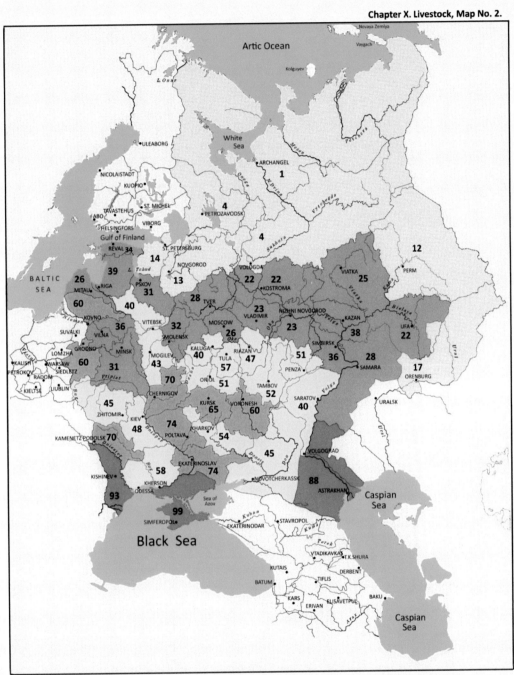

Based on the map from the Statistical Section of the Department of Agriculture and A. Jlyne S.P.B.

Number of large and small livestock per 100 dessiatines of fertile soil.

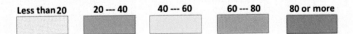

HORSES.

Based on the map from the Statistical Section of the Department of Agriculture and A. Jlyne S.P.B.

Number of horses in per cent of the total number of livestock.

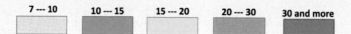

7 --- 10   10 --- 15   15 --- 20   20 --- 30   30 and more

LARGE-HORNED CATTLE.

Chapter X. Livestock, Map No. 4.

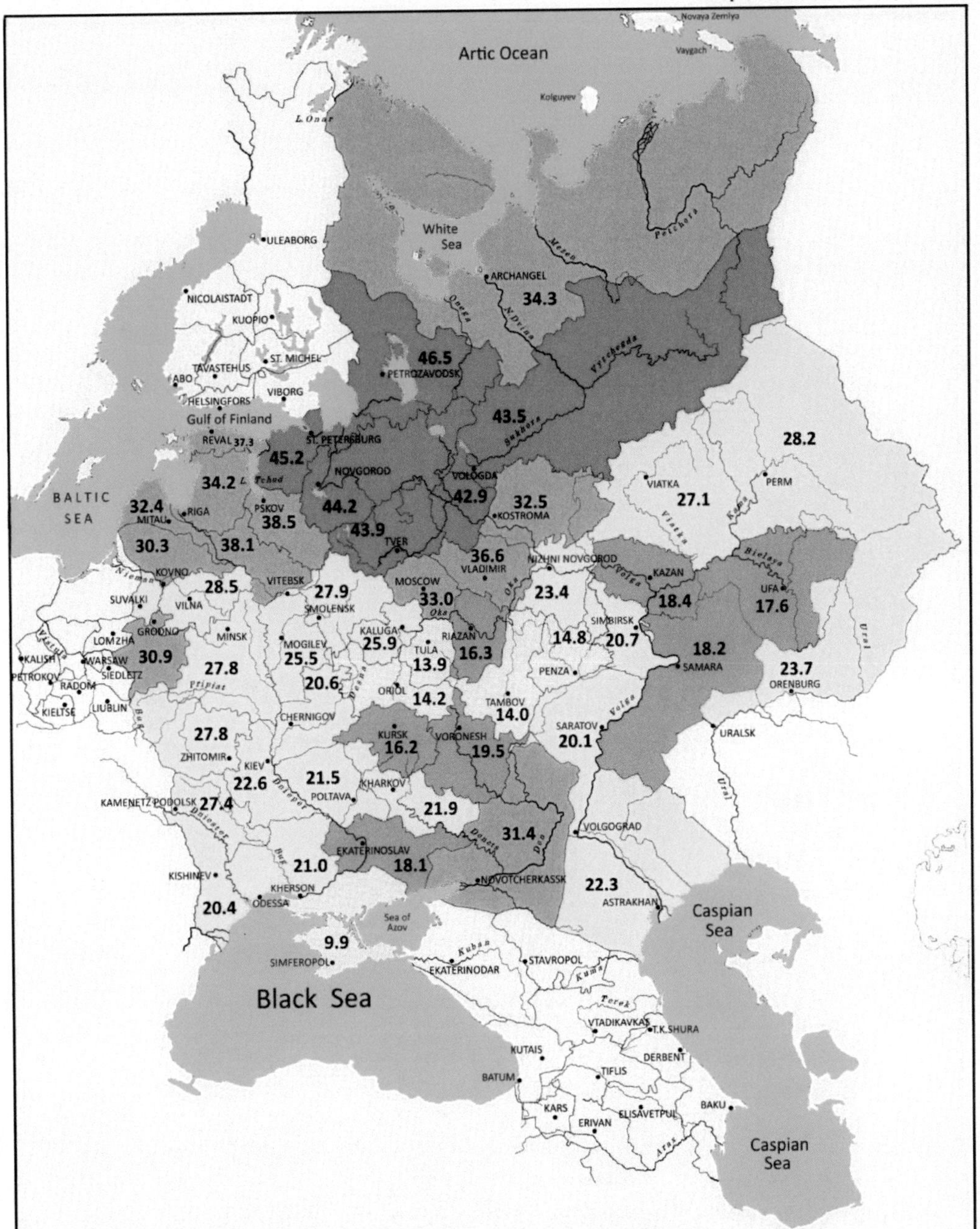

Based on the map from the Statistical Section of the Department of Agriculture and A. Jlyne S.P.B.

Number of large-horned cattle in per cent of the total number of livestock.

Less than 15	15 --- 20	20 --- 30	30 --- 40	40 or more

SHEEP.

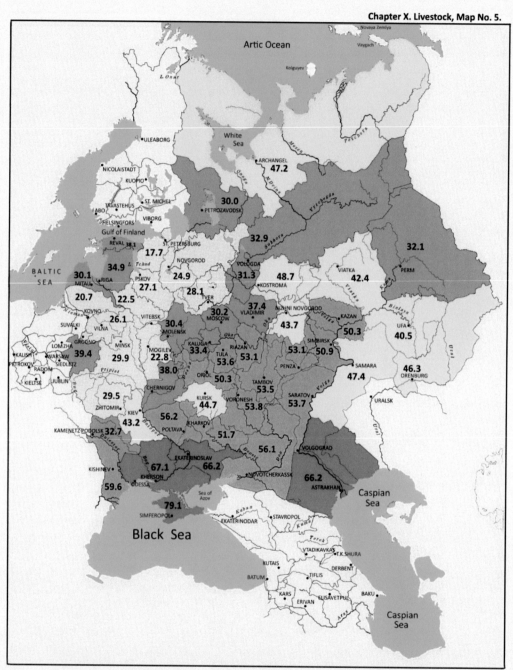

Number of sheep in per cent of the total number of livestock.

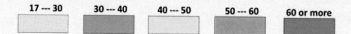

| 17 --- 30 | 30 --- 40 | 40 --- 50 | 50 --- 60 | 60 or more |

PIGS.

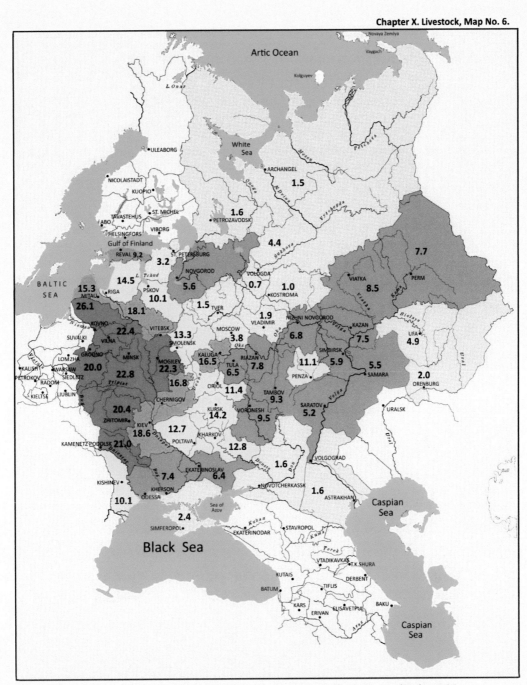

Based on the map from the Statistical Section of the Department of Agriculture and A. Jlyne S.P.B.

Number of pigs in per cent of the total number of livestock.

Less than 5%	5 --- 10%	10 --- 15%	15 --- 20%	More than 20%

Chapter XI. Rural Economy.

Highlights:

The price of land depends primarily on the profit that can be derived from the land. Map 1 shows the highest cost of land is in the non-steppe chernoziom region. There the population density and the rich soil allow substantial profits to be made from the production and selling of agricultural and animal products.

Map 2 shows how land prices have increased over the last three decades. In some places in Tauride, they have increased four or fivefold. The population increase and the coming of the railroad have helped support this increase.

"In the government of Samara land is very cheap, owing to the succession of bad crops during late years" (242).

"In general, land for the sowing of winter cereals is rented at a higher price than that for spring crops, except in those regions where the cultivation of spring wheat is especially general. The rent price of land for winter crops fluctuates from 3 to 25 roubles, in some cases amounting to 30 roubles per dessiatine; for spring sowings, farm rentals fluctuate from 3 to 20 roubles per dessiatine" (244).

"When land is rented for one season for some special crop, as for example, flax in the non-Chernoziom region, or for kitchen gardens and melon fields in the Chernoziom region, the price for land reaches its maximum, 40 to 50 roubles per dessiatine. When land is rented for a longer period the rental and selling prices are more nearly parallel to each other. The former vary from 4 to 6 per cent of the latter, and fluctuate from 50 kopecks to 15 roubles per dessiatine" (244).

"There are three different systems of hire in Russia: 1. by the year; 2. by the season or by the month; 3. by the day or by the job. The workmen hired by the year or by the season generally live on the estate and in addition to their monthly wages they are boarded and lodged. When they are hired by the day they are sometime given their meals, but more generally such expenses are deducted" (245).

"Workmen are often hired monthly, but still oftener for the summer, of about five months. This method of hire is practiced everywhere, more or less, and is the principal mode in sparsely populated localities of the Chernoziom region, where great numbers of workmen come from other places. As in the Chernoziom region, where the population is agricultural, the demand for workmen is much greater in summer than in winter, the wages paid to workmen hired for five months are excessively high, compared with those paid to the year workman. The summer hand receives generally about two-thirds of the wages paid to the labourer who is hired by the year and sometime more than that" (247–248).

In Koursk, a year workman gets about 55 roubles and a summer hand about 39 roubles. In Riazan those numbers are 51 and 35, respectively.

"In agricultural labour, daily workmen generally do the reaping, harvesting and thrashing; furthermore, they are hired for general work when the number of the year or summer hands, as well as of those hired by the job is insufficient" (248).

"There are two classes of daily workmen: simple hands, and those who furnish their own teams and instruments" (248).

"The wages paid to day labourers, who have their own teams and instruments, exceed that paid to simple hands from one-third to one-half. The same difference exists between the prices paid to men and to women. The average wages in spring during the sowing, are everywhere considerably lower than those paid during haymaking and cereal harvest" (248).

Tables on pages 246–247 and pages 249–250 of IR give the wages for workmen in the various governments of Russia. And tables on pages 253–255 analyze the potential costs and profits for the raising of various crops in the different regions and governments of European Russia.

"From these tables it may be seen that during the last five years the smallest profits, which in some localities did not even exceed the land rent, were produced from the principal Russian cereals, rye and oats, and nearly everywhere, especially in northern Russia, the cultivation of potatoes was most advantageous. In the south the greatest income was obtained by cultivating wheat, especially winter wheat, and to some extent barley" (256).

Growing conditions and markets are the greatest influence on the choices of crops. Nevertheless, estate owners tend to emphasize the profit motive while peasants emphasize growing food for their families.

Choices of Crops in Areas of Russia:

New Russia and southern steppes: Wheat has become the primary industry displacing the raising of sheep. Cattle raising and the sale of wool are even less important.

South-western governments: Beet growing and the production of sugar is of great importance.

Little Russia: Cereal production takes first place on estates as well as on peasant farms. All types of grain are of equal importance.

Central agricultural region: Rye and oats are the principal crops in this area.

Central Volga governments: Rye and oats are important here also as well as some cattle raising.

Lower Volga and eastern governments: Spring wheat and cattle as well as rye and other cereals are the primary crops for this region.

Moscow and neighboring governments: Flax for fiber, dairies, forestry and manufacturing industries are mainstays for the population.

Northwest: Peasants raise cereals and estate owners depend more on forestry.

Lake Region: Agriculture, cattle, milk production and forestry sustain the population.

"From the preceding it is easy to draw the conclusion that nearly over all the Chernoziom region farming, on the estates of landowners as well as on peasant farms, consists principally, if not exclusively, in the cultivation of cereals. Therefore, the good or bad crops have a decisive significance for the economical results of the year, on the landowners estates as well as on peasant farms" (259).

Remarks:

The numbers on Map 1 give the price of land in 1889 in roubles per dessiatine. To convert those prices to dollars per acre, divide by 2.6997 and multiply the exchange rate of 0.7752 dollars per rouble. Here is a small table based on that conversion:

Rouble per Dessiatine	Dollars per Acre
30	8.6
50	14.4
70	20.1
100	28.7
150	43.1

Map 2 shows the increase in prices for land from 1860 to 1889.

In Maps 3 and 4, the titles contain the words "for their board." For Map 3, I think that phrase is misleading and should be omitted. But I deferred to historical precedent and left the titles for both maps as they appear in IR.

Maps in other chapters also help to illuminate the statements and concepts in this chapter.

PRICES OF LAND IN 1889.

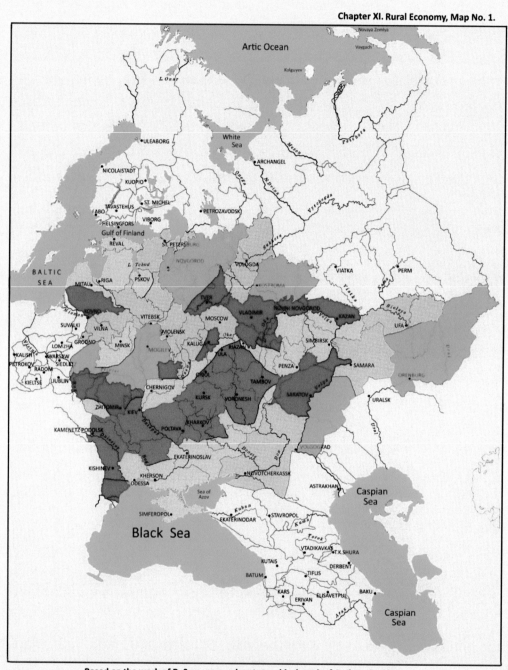

Chapter XI. Rural Economy, Map No. 1.

Based on the work of D. Semenov and cartographical work of A. Jlyne St. Pbg.

Average cost in roubles per Crown dessiatine in 1889.

| Less than 10 | 10 --- 30 | 30 --- 50 | 50 --- 70 | 70 --- 100 | More than 100 |

INCREASE IN THE PRICES OF LAND FROM 1860 TO 1889.

Chapter XI. Rural Economy, Map No. 2.

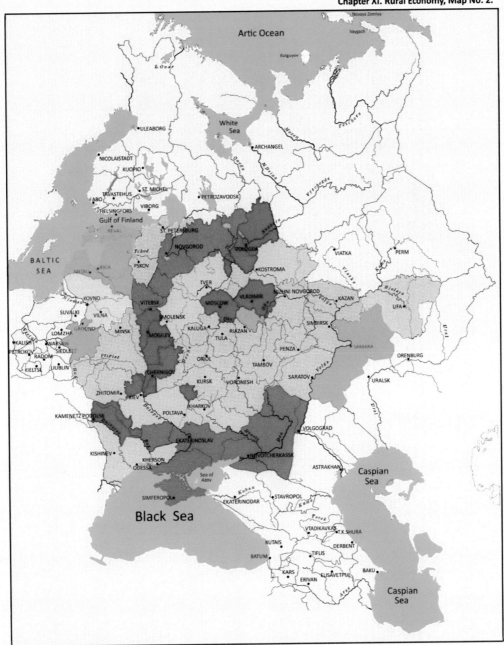

Based on the work of D. Semenov and cartographical works by A. Jlyne St. Pbg.

Increase in the selling price per dessiatine from the sixties to 1889.

| 50% or less | 50 --- 100% | 100 --- 150% | 150 --- 200% | 200 --- 300% | 300% or more |

YEARLY AVERAGE PRICES FROM 1882 TO 1891 ALLOWED IN HARVEST TIME TO DAY WORKMEN FOR THEIR BOARD.

Chapter XI. Rural Economy, Map No. 3.

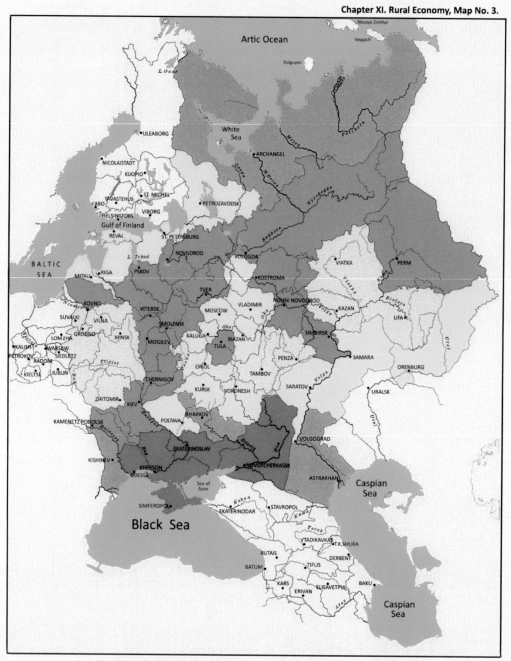

Based on the work of S. A. Korolenko and the cartographical work of A. Jlyne S.P.B.

| 41 --- 49 kopecks | 50 --- 59 kopecks | 63 --- 69 kopecks | 73 --- 84 kopecks | 1.07 --- 1.32 roubles |

FLUCTUATION OF THE AVERAGE PRICES FROM 1882 TO 1891 ALLOWED IN HARVEST TO DAY WORKMEN FOR THEIR BOARD.

Chapter XI. Rural Economy, Map No. 4.

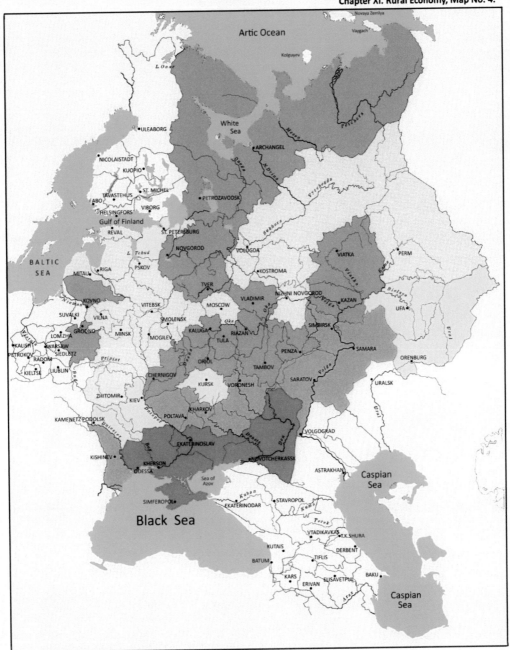

Based on the work of S. A. Korolenko and the cartographical work of A. Jlyne S.P.B.

| 5 --- 12 kopecks | 15 --- 20 kopecks | 25 --- 30 kopecks | 35 --- 70 kopecks | 1.55 -- 2.20 roubles |

Chapter XII. Farming Machines and Implements.

Highlights:

Ploughs:

The Russian sokha is made out of wood with two plow shares and a moldboard in the form of a triangle. The width of the triangle depends on the softness of the soil to be plowed. These plows are still widely used in the northern and non-chernoziom areas. The sokha costs 3 to 5 roubles.

In the southern steppes and chernoziom governments the Little Russian or colonist saban is used. It too is made out of wood but is very strong and 5 or 6 pairs of oxen can be hitched to it to plow to a depth of 3 or 4 vershocks (5 to 7 inches). These cost 7 to 10 roubles each.

"The German colonists, who immigrated to Russia at the end of the eighteenth century, have gradually improved this plough by making the moldboard, landside and the shoe of iron instead of wood, and by giving the share a more regular form. The chief peculiarity of this plough is that its landside is curved, owing to which it makes a broad furrow and keeps the grass from clogging it. As this implement is so general in Russia, the two celebrated English firms, Ransom, Sims & Jefferis, and Howard Brothers, constructed in 1875 a plough very similar to that of the colonists. Similar implements were also made in German factories, for example, by Ekkret, Fleter, Lenig and others. At the present time this perfected instrument has supplanted, on nearly all estates, the Little Russian and colonist ploughs" (264).

"In the southern steppe governments, owing to extensive arable lands and to the lack of workmen, a new method of ploughing has been introduced. It consists in joining three or four ploughs together, instead of using one simple implement; such a plough is called a boukker. With these compound ploughs the soil is upturned, immediately sown, and the seed covered with the aid of a drag call a ral; the latter consists of a massive wooden beam, to which 5 to 8 iron or wooden teeth are fixed. Sometimes a more simple process is followed: first the seed is sown and then covered with the boukker or the ral" (264).

Sowing:

"The sowing of fields is until now mostly by hand, and the seed is generally covered with simple harrows" (265).

Reaping:

"The cutting of grass and the reaping of grain is generally with scythes and cradles, principally imported from Austria. In the Tauride and Ekaterinoslav governments, owing to the influence of the German colonists, reaping machines made in the mechanical works belonging to the colonists themselves, were introduced in the sixties. These machines, called lobogreika or choubogreika, are constructed according to the ancient American type, made by Walter Wood, one of which was brought to Odessa in the fifties. Their construction has been gradually improved and now about 10,000 of them are made yearly" (265).

Thrashing:

"The thrashing of grain is by different methods, on many estates by thrashing machines of the English system, which were first constructed in Moscow by Wilson. These were the first machines of improved type introduced into Russia. Until now, in the different localities of the Empire, thrashing is done with the aid of horses, rollers, carts and other means. For these methods of thrashing, the sheaves are laid in a certain order and then from 3 to 6 horses are made to run over them, or carts, or wooden rollers, as in the governments of Yaroslav, Vladimir and Vologda, or rollers of iron, as in the steppe governments, are drawn over them" (265).

Winnowing and Cleaning:

"The grain is winnowed with the aid of a fanning mill, or simply with the spade and wind process, and is finally cleaned on a peculiar leathern sieve or with cylindrical sorters, with a system of wire screens. In the southern governments the colonist winnowing machines are very much used. They are of a special construction and sieves in them move backwards and forwards, and therefore clean the grain very rapidly. The above mentioned implements and machines are until now used by peasants, German colonist and Cossacks, partly also by the estate owners" (265).

Manufacturing, Repairing and Selling Machinery:

"The principal centres of trade in farming implements and machines are Rostov-on-Don, Odessa, Kharkov, Kiev, Moscow, Warsaw, Riga, Saratov, Samara and St. Petersburg; Rostov-on-Don occupies the first place, as it is now one of the principal points in south Russia which supplies the two richest regions of Kouban and Tersk and the government of Stavropol with faming machines. There are 6 large and 5 small depots in that town. The greatest number of portable engines and steam thrashers, of which, in 1888, 400 were imported valued at 2,500,000 roubles, are taken by the south. The first depots for farming machines were established in St. Petersburg, Moscow, Warsaw, Kharkov and Odessa" (267).

"The United States of America made Russia acquainted with their machines and began to export them into the Empire only since 1876, when, owing to the Centennial Exposition at Philadelphia some Russian specialists were able closely to examine the excellent qualities of the American machinery. Until that year the Americans, principally Wood, Mac Cormick, Osborn and others, sent into Russia only reaping machines, and had to compete with the English makes. But since 1876, drills and planters, spring harrows, mowing machines, binders, horse rakes, and hay presses have been imported from America, and in this line the latter has no rival in Russia. American reapers, mowing machines and horse rakes have quite supplanted the English types; American drills have taught the Russian farmers to sow in rows, and the American hay presses are regarded as models;

but ploughs of American construction are not used in Russia, only because they are too expensive; as to their quality, they occupy the first place" (267).

"In examining the separate categories of the machine industry in Russia the production of ploughs must be put in the first place, and considered as the triumph of the industry. The progress made in the manufacture and construction of is very considerable in the last ten years. The first plough of improved type made its appearance at the Moscow Exhibition in 1882, but since then their number has greatly increased. Workshops producing especially constructed ploughs were formerly very rare, but there are now numbers of them, the leading firms being John Hoene, Jacob Hoene, F. Helle in Odessa, Donski Brothers in Nikolaev, the Votkinsk Crown Manufactory, the Riazan Co., and Ganshin and Co. in Yaroslav. The demands for ploughs increase yearly and have developed to such an extent that, for instance, in Rostov-on-Don, the trade in them can be compared to that of articles of first necessity. In an ordinary year about 10,000 ploughs are sold, and when the crops are very good, many more; the same holds good in Moscow" (269).

"The manufacture of reaping machines called lobogreika and choubogreika, is especially developed in Russia. They are made at the mechanical works belonging to colonists, in the governments of Ekaterinoslav, Tauride and Kherson, and also in the factories in Kharkov, Elisavetgrad, Berdiansk, Marioupol and in other towns. Seven or eight years ago this industry was not much developed, but latterly it has attained great proportions. In summer, 7,000 to 8,000 pieces are sold yearly, and when the crops are good, considerably more, so that the manufacture of reapers in southern Russia may be considered as second only to that of ploughs. Trials have been made of producing such reapers as throw off the grain in bundles; the prices of such machines are remarkably low" (269).

"In the production of complicated thrashing machines, and especially in those working by steam, Russia is still far in the rear of other nations. Until now they are being imported, which is explained by the fact that the Russian builders cannot get dry wood of good quality, and have not enough money to carry a stock of seasoned lumber" (270).

Remarks:

Chapter V of this book covers some of the same topics as this chapter.

A hay press is the precursor to a baler that makes square bales.

German colonists are mentioned a number of times in this chapter and other chapters of IR. They lived in the southern tier of governments in European Russia as well as along the Volga River in Saratov and Samara provinces.

They came to Russia at the invitation of Catherine the Great and Alexander I. Two migrations followed their invitations, the first in 1763–68 and the second approximately in the years 1803–1820 (Bosch 10–18, 45–49). They were granted special privileges including free land and exemption from the draft. But in the late 1800s other Russians became increasingly envious of their special treatment and their relative prosperity. In 1871, their special status began to be revoked and in 1874 their young males became subject to the draft.

Despite the hatred of all things German sweeping Russia at the time, these people are given credit in IR for helping develop agriculture and associated industries in Russia. Had the political climate been more favorable, I believe they would have received still more attention and credit in IR.

Chapter XIII. Agricultural Schools.

Highlights:

The first agricultural schools were founded in the 1820s and their mission was to prepare young men to manage estates. These early schools were generally unsuccessful because the peasant boys soon reverted back to the old familiar methods of farming and the boys from the nobility class took advantage of their education and entered government.

Progress and achievement of goals was usually slow at these schools. An exception seems to be the Petrovsk Academy of Agriculture and Forestry established near Moscow in 1865.

"Thus, since 1882 there are seven middle agricultural schools in Russia, all of which not only prepare managers for private estates, but also answer many other practical and educational purposes. The students after finishing the course in these institutions either become estate bailiffs, teachers in lower agricultural schools, or after post graduate study become specialists in the different branches of agriculture, as for example, in gardening, flax cultivation, tobacco growing, wine making, milk farming, stock raising, et cetera" (278).

Classes in surveying land began in 1858 in the Gorigoretsk Agricultural Institution.

Schools to prepare gardeners and wine makers began in 1869. Between 1871 and 1881 six lower agricultural schools were established. The first was set up in Tver.

"The school admitted pupils of both sexes without any restriction as to age or qualifications, those who had finished their course in higher schools, as well as those who did not know how to read or write" (283).

Dairy schools were also set up. A couple of them admitted only girls.
"Into these schools are received girls not younger than 16, and who must previously have gone through the regular course of studies at one of the national

schools. They are instructed in those branches of rural and domestic industry with which women have generally [had] to occupy themselves, namely: the management of the dairy, bird breeding, gardening, kitchen gardening, cooking sewing, nursing, et cetera" (286).

Many or all of these agricultural schools have land associated with them so students can gain some practical experience to go with their theoretical work.

Remarks:

The Russian schools appear to have had problems well-known to current educators namely: poorly prepared students and less than optimal support from the government. Reorganization and the closing of schools seem to have been common occurrences.

Map 1 gives the location of agricultural, forestry and mining schools in European Russia.

SCHOOLS UNDER THE JURISDICTION
OF THE MINISTRY OF DOMAINS.

Chapter XIII. Agricultural schools.

Based on cartographical works of A. Jlyne ST. PBG.

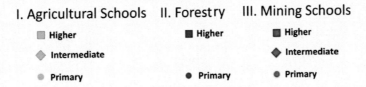

I. Agricultural Schools   II. Forestry   III. Mining Schools

- Higher
- Intermediate
- Primary

- Higher
- Primary

- Higher
- Intermediate
- Primary

Chapter XIV. Industrial Rural Credit.

Highlights:

Banks for lending money to people of nobility were established as early as 1754. Later on banks were set up to help peasants buy land. In 1820, a Count Arakcheev founded a bank to make loans to peasants. By 1876, the Alexandrovsk Bank was allowed to buy and sell "papers bearing interest" and to receive deposits.

"Inasmuch as the bank effected its principal operations on short-termed deposits, and placed them out on advances extending over long periods, it was only natural that, should any great run be made on the bank deposits, it would have extreme difficulty in meeting the demands made upon it. This is exactly what happened in the year 1891, and the bank must have suspended payments, if it had not received help from the Government, which took upon itself to satisfy the claims of the depositors, and undertook the management of the bank by drawing up temporary rules for its administration, these rules to remain in force only till the bank should be completely reorganized and set on a firm and lasting footing" (292).

The emancipation of the serfs in1861, stimulated the creation of financial products and induced stresses throughout European Russia. Sometimes loans were advanced for agricultural produce. In 1881, an idea was floated to make loans to purchase machines but was not implemented.

"Thus, in 1815, was formed the New Russian Fund for Rural Industry, amounting in all to about 500,000 roubles. The fund was designed the advancement of loans for the sake of promoting improvements in certain branches of rural industry in the Taurid, Kherson, Ekaterinoslav and Bessarabian governments"(309).

"A special fund of 60,000 roubles was also formed for advancing loans on drainage works in the Taurid government. The interest on loans was fixed at 4 per cent yearly. All expenses incurred by loans, or the valuation and inspection of works on which they were advanced, fell on the borrowers. The loans were advanced for periods extending from 1 to 10 years. The greater part of the sums thus obtained was expended on boring artesian wells, constructing dykes, digging canals, et cetera" (309).

Remarks:

Some of the terms for loans were as follows (291): Four percent interest and two percent for liquidation of the term of 28 years. It is possible that they meant there should be a fixed payment of 6% of the original loan to be allocated to 4% interest and the rest to the reduction of the principal. This would discharge the loan in 28 annual payments.

It is interesting to note then as now, in Russia as well as in the US, banks got into financial trouble and the government had to bail them out (see the first quote in this chapter).

This chapter is very technical but a person interested in the history of finance and banking in Russia can find a lot of material here.

Chapter XV. Forestry.

Highlights:

The forests of Russia are natural not planted by humans. In the north there are more trees but not as many species of trees as in the south.

Only a few species are widespread and they are pine, spruce, fir, oak, birch, trembling poplar and linden. Pine, spruce and fir grow primarily in northern Russia. Beech grows in the south and southwestern parts of Russia. Oak trees grow over the northern parts of Russia but not in the steppe region.

Winter oak grows in the governments of Kiev, Poltava, Kharkov, Voronezh and Crimea. Another variety grows in Volyn, Podolsk, Bessarabia, Crimea and in the Caucasus. Elm trees also grow in western Russia, Crimea and the Caucasus. Linden tree grow over much of Russia but not in the steppes.

Pine and fir comprise about 61% of the lumber cut in Russia, birch 10%, oak 9% and other deciduous trees the remainder.

Scientific forest management has started in just the last three decades.

Some the wood in Russia is used to power railroad and steamboat engines. By 1891, however, mineral fuel surpassed the use of wood for those purposes. At the present time ship building, mining and manufacturing use more wood than railroads and steamboats. Altogether Russia uses at least 7.5 million cubic sagenes (2572.5 million cubic feet) of timber.

In 1888 laws were passed which are intended to preserve trees in critical areas and which regulate the conversion of forest land into arable land.

A large number of home industries are based on making articles from wood. The list includes carriage makers, joiners, coopers, wheelwrights and furniture makers. Other articles fashioned from wood are utensils, shaft bow, small and large sleighs, cording combs, spinning wheels and looms, harrows, packing trunks, window frames, doors, coffins, toys, musical instruments, tobacco boxes, some wooden shoes (called bast shoes) and bast twine. Pitch and tar are also made from trees.

Remarks:

Tables on pages 322–325 of IR give some information about areas that are forested as well as total area of governments. Here is a small extraction of those tables for southern Russia and the southern Volga region (areas are given in geographical square miles):

Government	Number of Inhabitants in thousands	Total area of dry land	Total area of forest land	Percent that is forest
Bessarabia	1773	816	51.4	6.3
Don Region	1852	2868	30.2	1.1
Ekaterinoslav	2096	1211	11.2	0.9
Kherson	2352	1275	11.6	0.9
Samara	2826	2703	144.6	5.3
Saratov	2581	1512	154.8	10.2
Tauride	1230	1082	39.3	3.6

A geographical square mile equals 21.25 square English miles or 55.06 square kilometers.

A cubic sagene equals 343 cubic feet.

Chapter XVI. Goods Freights in Conjunction with Transport Statistics.

Highlights:

The rates of Russian railroad companies have always been regulated. In 1861 relevant statutes governed rates for the Chief Company of Russian Railways and for nearly all other rail companies. Here are some of the rates:

First class passengers: 3 kopecks per verst.
Second class passenger: 2¼ kopecks per verst.
Third class passenger: 1¼ kopecks per verst.
Allowance of 1 poud of luggage free per passenger, extra luggage is charged at the rate of 1/20 kopeck per verst for every 10 pounds.
Working cattle (oxen, cows, bulls, horses and mules): 3 kopecks per verst.
Calves and swine: 1 kopeck per verst.
Rams, sheep, lambs, goats and dogs: ½ kopeck per verst.

For slow goods trains, first class goods ship at 1/12 of a kopeck per verst; second class at 1/18 kopeck per verst and third class goods at 1/24 kopeck per verst. **See Remarks.**

First class goods are items such as iron and lead wares, copper, cast iron, metals both wrought and unwrought, cotton yarn, wine, tea, coffee and so on. There are 52 items on this list.

Second class goods include ores, charcoal, cotton, pig iron, flax, hemp, cloth and linen and so on for a total of 44 articles.

Third class items are corn, flour, vegetables, salt, lime, sand and so on for 34 items.

The lists above do not include everything that is shipped on railroads and other items are to be compared to items on the list and priced in a comparable fashion.

The government has exercised little oversight on the railroads. In addition, the rates above are quite high which has led to pricing wars between competing rail companies. As a consequence a myriad of pricing policies and rates have come about.

"Hence arose such complication of the accounts of the lines, both with those who forwarded the goods and with other lines, that not only the public, but even the railway agents themselves, had the utmost difficulty in disentangling the confusion, and they constantly fell into errors which resulted in mutual recrimination, complaints and disputes" (354).

In addition various special allowance are made for grain, salt, iron goods, mineral fluids, kerosene, sugar, sugar beets, cattle, horses, wood and so on.

"The introduction of a common tariff on all these lines, which took place on January 1, 1893, was therefore an important step towards the ultimate adoption of one common schedule on all the Russian railways, to which end it was in fact a preliminary step" (364).

The total length of Russian railways is about 32,000 versts.

In 1889 the total amount of grain transported over the whole Russian railroads was 497 million pouds. In 1890, the amount was 485 million pouds. Those quantities were distributed over the following destinations (in thousands of pouds) (365):

Ports	1889	1890
Odessa	46,931	51.652
St. Petersburg	30,109	38,246
Libau	39,885	34,185
Riga	21,236	28,211
Sebastopol	28,382	13,887
Novorossisk	20,336	32,468

Rostov-on-Don	17,554	14,038
Reval	14,369	13,447
Taganrog	6,470	8,334
Marioupol	3,010	3,562
Poti	1,443	2,189
Batoum	654	328
Genichesk	291	818

Frontier Points:

Sosnovitsi	7,042	5,812
Alexandrovo	4,128	4,076
Volochisk	4,182	2,568
Radzivilov	2,208	1,505

Interior Points:

Moscow	31,220	32,923
Warsaw	9,323	7,676
Samara	6,504	7,529
Saratov	7,906	6,021
Kiev	2,603	2,800
Tiflis	2,535	2,606

Remarks:

I believe the rates for slow goods trains were in kopecks per poud per verst. The authors of IR left out the "per poud" on page 353.

Slow goods trains are probably what we call freight trains in the US.

Pages 364–384 give a very detailed account of amount of shipping and rates for shipping over European Russia in the 1880–93 period.

Chapter XVII. Household Industry.

Highlights:

Wood is the material used in trades such as carriage building, coopering and joinery. Distillation of wood yields products such as pitch, tar and potash. Wheels and carts are sold at fairs and bazaars.

"Sometimes the coopers sell their manufactures at the bazaars, and in the northern Volga governments they are bought by middlemen, who transport them to wholesale dealers in the southern Volga governments" (386).

Cabinet makers make as little as 40 roubles per year to as much as 100 or 500 roubles for the more skilled and owners of shops (386-387). Bent chairs are made from branches of wild cherry trees and a dozen may fetch six roubles. A dozen armchairs may bring 8–12 roubles.

Hemp is used to make fish nets especially in Nizhni-Novgorod.

"In the government of Saratov, where the sarpinka is mainly worked, weavers earn from 33 to 45 kopecks per day, and from 50 to 60 roubles per year" (389).

Boots and shoes of varying quality are made from dressed hides. "The boots and shoes are bought on the village markets, and bazaars, by the middlemen and spread over all Russia" (389).

Sheepskin clothes are made for warmth. The fair at Nizhni-Novgorod attracts sellers of these coats.

"The earnings of the lace makers are very insignificant; working 18 hours per day a woman earns 20 kopecks, and not more than 35 roubles for the whole season" (393).

Other kustars (peasant handicraftsmen and women) make pottery items, forge nails and knives, fashion fishhooks and manufacture firearms and sidearms.

Remarks:

Chapter XVII in IR gives a very interesting account of the cottage industries that sprang up in rural Russia to service agricultural and consumer needs. Much of this work was seasonal, that is when it was too cold to do field work. The following table shows some of the wages that were earned by a craftsman (Kustar). There are 100 kopecks per rouble.

Trade	Wage/Per Time Period
Cooper	30-40 kopecks per day in season
Joiner	90-100 roubles/year; 100-500 roubles/year in larger towns
Basket maker	20-60 kopecks/day; 20 roubles/year
Mat maker	40 roubles/year
Pitch boiler	30 roubles/season
Spoon maker	15-20 kopecks/day
Weavers	70-100 roubles/season
Sarpinka weavers	50-60 roubles/year
Shoemakers	30-100 kopecks/day (This was one of the highest paying jobs.)
Sheepskin maker	16 roubles/month
Silk weaver	120-200 roubles/year
Potter	2-3 roubles/week
Nail forger	1.5-2 roubles/week
Tack maker	5-7 roubles/week (Near population centers like Moscow.)
Fishhook maker	10-30 kopecks/day
Toy maker	50-120 or more roubles/year

Compare these wages with the price of a bushel of wheat by checking Diagrams 1a and 1b in Chapter VII.

Chapter XVIII. Manufactures from Farm Produce.

Highlights:

Farming mills are prevalent over all of Russia. Commercial grinding mills are mainly used for the grinding of wheat.

"In the end of the sixties the first mill with rollers for grinding flour was established in Russia, in Kazan by Romanov Brothers; this example showing brilliant results was soon followed by many large mill owners of the Volga region" (395).

In 1884 the fall of prices for breadstuffs and flour brought the expansion of flour production to a halt.

". . . Russia consumes yearly 82 million chetverts of rye and 18 million chetverts of wheat in the form of bread" (396).

The flour industry in Russia is centered about the mills of the Volga region which produces about 40% of the total.

"The largest and most perfect mills are situated in towns. Odessa produces about four and a half million pouds; Rostov-on-Don, three and half million pouds; Kremenchoug, Elisavetgrad and Ekaterinoslav, 3 million pouds each; Kiev, 2 millions; Sebastopol, 1,500,000, and Kerch about one million pouds yearly" (397).

Mills generally were built along waterways at first but as railroads came into being, mills began to be built along the railways.

About 2.5 million pouds of flour is exported by Russia yearly. About 60% of the export comes through the Veinstein mill in Odessa.

Other products made from flour are starch, molasses and brandy.

"The first factory for the making of molasses was founded in 1826 in St. Petersburg by Shoulz, a foreigner" (403).

Chemical methods for getting starch from wheat are the Elsass method and the Marten method (403).

Remarks:

The first paragraph and fourth paragraph in the highlights section appear to be in contradiction.

A Russian chetvert is equivalent to 5.9567 American bushels and a Russian poud is equivalent to 32.243 English or American pounds.

Kremenchough (Kremenchug) is a town on the Dnieper River in the Government of Poltava .

Elisavetgrad is a town in what is now central Ukraine. Ekaterinoslav is now called Dnepropetrovsk and is in present-day Ukraine.

Chapter XIX. Fish and Other Marine Animals.

Highlights:

At one time fish were extremely abundant all over the Russian Empire. But as civilization developed, forests were cut and steppes plowed, the fisheries in the middle and upper parts of streams and rivers declined, especially in European Russia. Thus the fishing industry is now concentrated near the mouths of rivers and the seas. Nevertheless, the lakes and streams still produce large quantities of fish for local consumption.

The fishing industry:

The fishing industry can be divided into the following six regions with the main species of fish as listed:

1. The Caspian–Volga Region: Sturgeon, sterlet, salmon[salmo caspius], herring, vobla, sander, bream, carp, taran, perch and pike. From these fish the industry produces caviar, cod liver oil and salted, dried and pickled fish.

2. Azov Sea Area: This fishery is very similar to the Caspian–Volga fishery but does not include salmon.

3. Black Sea Region: Sturgeon, kefal, scomber and herring. Products from this fishery include caviar, canned fish, salted, smoked and dried fish.

4. Baltic Sea Region: German sturgeon, salmon[salmo salar], pilchard, sprat, taimen, spurling and herring. Products from this fishery include caviar and canned or fresh fish.

5. Frozen and White Sea District: Salmon[salmo trutta], trout, cod, herring, turbot and wolf fish. These fish are sold fresh or frozen.

6. River and Lake Fisheries: Salmon, perch, carp and sturgeon are caught and used locally. The principal methods of preservation are salting, air drying, oven drying and canning.

"The most valuable of these preserves is the caviar of the sturgeon. Immediately after the eggs have been removed they are rubbed through a sieve, slightly salted, put into tin jars, and are then ready for sale. When thus prepared the caviar is called fresh or zernistaia, and is rather dear. Another sort of this product, called payusnaia, is cheaper; it is cured in salted water and then pressed in bags" (414).

Sea Animals:

Whales, dolphins and seals are sea animals of some importance. From 40,000 to 80,000 seals are killed annually by Russian hunters in the White Sea and Northern Ocean.

Methods of Fishing:

The mesh of fishing nets is usually made of hemp or flax yarn. Eisk and Taganrog on the Azov Sea have the only two factories making nets. The nets in the rest of Russia are usually made by the fishermen themselves or by peasants in nearby villages.

In some areas a long line with multiple secondary lines with hooks are used. **Remark:** In the US, this is called a set line.

Fishing hooks are made in the village Bezvodvoe in the district of Nizhni-Novgorod.

"On the Volga a special instrument, called shashkovaia snast, is used for catching the sterlet [a small sturgeon]; it has hooks standing downwards. The sterlet is also caught with common fishing rods, and with earth worms as bait" (420).

"A very ingenious implement is used on the Volga for fishing white fish (belorybitsa); it is called sidebka and is so constructed, that the fish caught is instantly thrown out on the ice" (420).

Remarks:

I believe the instrument described in the previous paragraph is also described in more detail in Gmelin (156,169).

The salmon, salmo caspius and salmo truttus, mentioned in this chapter may also be called Caspian Trout or Sea Trout, respectively. The salmon[salmon salar] is a species of Atlantic Salmon.

Chapter XX. Rural Industries of the Caucasus.

Highlights:

The Caucasus Mountains run roughly from Sochi on the Black Sea to Baku on the Caspian Sea. The highest point is about 18,500 feet above sea level and the Caspian Sea is below sea level.

The region north of the Caucasus Mountains is known as the Northern Caucasus and the part south of those mountains is known as Transcaucasia. The provinces on Map B belonging to the Northern Caucasus are Derbent (69), Terek(77), Kuban (70) and Stavropol (75). The other governments are part of Transcaucasia.

Agriculture is the primary industry in the Caucasus. Wheat and barley are the main grains grown but rye and spelt are also seen. Western Transcaucasia gets plenty of rain. Corn, olives and lemon grow there. Eastern Transcaucasia, on the other hand, is dry and hot. Irrigation is used to grow crops such as rice, tobacco, apricots, peaches and almonds. A variety of melons are also grown here. Apples and pears appear throughout the region. Vineyards support wine making but only in areas where Christians are in the majority.

Nomadic and semi-nomadic tribes raise sheep and cattle in the Northern Caucasus but cultivation of crops is gradually replacing their means of existence. Cattle are also raised in western Transcaucasia but sheep and goats are more prominent in eastern Transcaucasia. A few camels and buffalo appear especially in eastern Transcaucasia.

"Buffalo breeding is, for the most part, limited to low lying places, since they are unable to support the cold. These animals replace oxen and cows in ploughing the land; they have great draught power, and give a milk which in many places is valued more highly than cow milk; in a word, their good qualities completely redeem any defects they may have" (442).

The soil in the northern Caucasus area is rich and rainfall generally adequate. Thus it is becoming one of the breadbaskets of European Russia and, in case of crop failure elsewhere, can supply grain for export.

Remarks:

The Caucasus referred to in IR are now Azerbaijan, Georgia and Armenia.
This region as described in IR appears to have an appealing array of geography and climatic conditions. Unfortunately, it is also subject to political and ethnic strife.

Chapter XXI. Rural Industries and Forestry of Turkestan.

Highlights:

Turkestan may be divided into two parts: the first is the area which can be irrigated by water from rivers or from smaller streams lying at the foot of mountains or which can be irrigated from scattered oases. This watered area consists of at most 2.5% of the total. The rest of the country is steppe land which supports nomadic people whose main occupation is herding.

A variety of grains and other crops are grown on irrigated ground. These include wheat, barley, oats, rice, cotton, millet, flax, sorghum, melons as well as other field and garden crops. Fruits such as apples, pears, plums, cherries, apricots and peaches and nuts such as almonds, walnuts and pistachio are grown domestically and also harvested from wild trees especially at the higher elevations.

"Under favorable circumstances, the winter wheat sowings yield good crops, far in excess of those obtained in European Russia and in the United States. On an average, one dessiatine yields from 120 to 140 pouds (12 to 14 chetverts), of winter wheat, and in exceptional cases as much as 160 or 200 pouds" (454).

"Without any exaggeration, Turkestan may be called the land of apricots and peaches. An enormous quantity of these and other fruits, both when fresh as well as after they have been dried in the sun, is consumed by the population, whilst a brisk trade is done with the nomads in dried peaches and apricots" (462).

Grapes are also grown and either eaten fresh or dried into raisins. Only where Russians have established themselves in later years have any of the grapes been used to make wine.

Other garden crops are melons, watermelons, pumpkins, onions, turnips, tomatoes, cabbage and so on.

". . . but only a few of these are grown in large quantities, or rank among the important produce of the country. To such plants belong melons, watermelons, cucumbers, pumpkins, carrots and onions. The first place among the latter plants must be assigned to melons, which are grown everywhere in large quantities and form the principal food article for the natives in the summer season" (460–461).

There is some dry land farming that depends on timely rains which are often missing. The primary dry land crops are spring wheat, spring barley and millet.

The best soil in Turkestan is in river valleys and along the forelands of mountain ranges. The latter is called "wood soil" and is extremely rich and capable of producing great crops provided sufficient rain or water can be applied to the plants.

Natives eat primarily mutton and horse flesh for meat and little beef. Sheep are the main animals bred in Turkestan. The cattle are used as draft animals, pack animals and as producers of milk. Sometimes the Kirghiz use bulls as saddle animals.

Nomads don't store much for their animals for the winter months and as a consequence sometimes lose a large part of their flocks to severe weather.

Camels are sensitive to rain and cold and so nomads do put up a store of reeds and steppe grass for these animals.

"Among the nomads, camel breeding is an important branch of the live-stock industry, and though of late the introduction of railroads into the Transcaspian province has caused a considerable decline in their number, still even now the camel, by the reason of its strength, endurance, and the ease with which it can be reared on any fodder, continues to be the sole means of transporting goods over the enormous steppes, and through the wastes of Central Asia" (467).

Around oases, the ass is the choice for a beast of burden.

"The pacification of the country under Russian rule, the great increase in the quantity of land cultivated by settled residents, the murrain among the cattle, produced by frosts, the expulsion of the nomads by new settlers in places suitable for a regular mode of life, and many other secondary causes have had for their result a gradual decline in cattle breading over the whole extent of the steppes of Turkestan" (464).

Forests in Turkestan appear only in mountainous areas and river valleys and eons of over-cutting has reduced even those tracts to a great degree.

In 1888, the Transcaspian railroad was opened linking Samarcand with the Caspian Sea. This will have a profound effect on all aspects of life in Turkestan.

Remarks:

Turkestan lies just east of the Caspian Sea. It coincides roughly with present-day Kazakhstan, Uzbekistan and Turkmenistan. Transcaspia corresponds approximately to Turkmenistan and southwestern Kazakhstan.

To convert pouds of wheat per dessiatine to bushels per acre, multiply by 32.243, divide that result by 60 and then divide by 2.6997. If we do that, we can restate the yields in the highlights above as follows:

Pouds per Dessiatine	Bushels per Acre
120	24
140	28
160	32
200	40

Maps of Turkestan can be found at the following website:
http://www.lib.utexas.edu/maps/commonwealth/turkmenistan_physio-2008.jpg

Chapter XXII. Government Measures for the Protection of Rural Industries.

Highlights:

"The first serious attempt to develop and protect the rural industries of Russia by means of direct Government measures was made in the reign of Peter the Great (1689–1725). The active interference of the Emperor, who brought his personal energy to bear on every branch of Imperial government, was chiefly directed to the extension of agriculture to the numerous parts of the Empire that then lay waste and idle, and to the introduction of the cultivation of new species of plants and domestic animals into farming households. At a later period, the pursuits of the rural population were the object of special solicitude on the part of the Government throughout the reign of Catherine the Second (1762–1796). In those years the Government inaugurated not a few measures that were calculated to have a great influence on the future of Russian agriculture. Of these measures the most important was the law decreeing a general land survey and the establishment of fixed boundaries, by which the security of landed property was guaranteed, and the development of rural industries was placed on a firm and solid basis. Equally important was the invitation given to foreign colonists to come over and settle in Russia, with the object of bringing under cultivation the sparsely inhabited districts of the Empire, and of improving the primitive system of agriculture hitherto adopted by the native population" (472).

In 1802 the Ministry of the Interior was given jurisdiction over all agricultural affairs.

In 1834 chairs of rural economy were established at universities and agricultural associations started forming as early as 1765 in St. Petersburg. The work of those associations have been helped by the emancipation of the serfs in 1861 and the development of the railroads in the latter half of the 1880s.

The ministry of Imperial Domains and the Department of Agriculture and Rural Industry superseded the Ministry of the Interior in 1837.

"In order to collect information on the actual condition of rural industries, the Agricultural Department, following the example of the United States, applies directly to village landed proprietors and farmers. The latter, in all from 4,500 to 6,000 correspondents at appointed periods, generally five time a year, forward to the Department information as to the grain and grass crops, cattle breeding, labour wages, the market price of rural products, changes made in the cultivation of land, and the actual condition of the various branches of rural industry" (475).

The Agriculture Department publishes surveys on conditions of crops during and after the growing season and promotes agricultural exhibitions.

The Agricultural Gazette is a weekly paper that has been published since 1834. Farming and Forestry is a monthly magazine and started publication in 1841.

The government has led efforts to build reservoirs and canals in order to demonstrate the potential of irrigation in the dry areas of the southern and south-eastern steppes. In the northeast, the government has begun drainage projects to recover and make productive land now occupied by swamps and bogs.

Other government initiatives include promoting the use of artificial fertilizers, the widespread use of better cereal seeds, the betterment of cattle breeds, the cultivation of silkworms and the improvement of fishery stocks especially in the central areas of Russia.

Zemstva also work to distribute agricultural knowledge and introduce new methods and machinery for improving the raising of produce. They have started elementary schools to train students in aspects of rural industries. Some facilitate the purchase of machinery and mineral fertilizers. Others have begun a rotating seed program in which farmers are given new seed and they return a somewhat greater amount after the harvest in order to continue the process. Generally, Zemstva concern themselves with all aspects of local governance and all areas of concern of the local population.

Remarks:

Catherine the Second was also known as Catherine the Great.

Zemstva is the plural form of zemstvo. Zemstva were introduced by legislation in 1864. They very gradually took over the local governing functions and drew power away from foreign colonists such as the Germans. In 1871 the special status of the German villages was revoked and they were placed under the zemstva form of local governance (Giesinger 224–226).

Works Cited and Other References

Bosch, William. *The German-Russians in Words and Pictures.* Spearfish, South Dakota. 2015. Print.

Crawford, John Martin, ed. *The Industries of Russia, Volume III: Agriculture and Forestry.* St. Petersburg, Russia. 1893. Print.

Crawford, John Martin, ed. *The Industries of Russia, Volume III: Agriculture and Forestry.* 1893. Google Book Search. Web. 10 November 2016.

<https://books.google.com/books?id=_dZDAAAAYAAJ&dq=The+Industries+of+Russia,+Volume+3&source=gbs_navlinks_s>

Ediger, Glen. *Leave No Threshing Stone Unturned.* North Newton, Kansas. 2012. Print.

Giesinger, Adam. *From Catherine to Khrushchev: The Story of Russia's Germans.* Lincoln: The American Historical Society of Germans from Russia. 1981. Print.

Gmelin, Samuel G. *Astrakhan Anno 1770: Its History, Geography, Population, Trade, Flora, Fauna and Fisheries.* Trans. Willem Floor. Washington: Mage, 2013. Print.

Industries of Russia, Volume 3. ULAN Press. 2016. Print.

IR. See Crawford.

Moon, David. *The Plough that Broke the Steppes: Agriculture and Environment on Russia's Grasslands, 1700–1914.* Oxford University Press. 2013. Print

INDEX

This index does not reference anything on the maps or diagrams in this book. Use the Table of Contents for a guide to the maps and diagrams.

Made in the USA
Middletown, DE
21 April 2017